1st EDITION

Perspectives on Modern World History

The End of Apartheid

1st EDITION

Perspectives on Modern World History

The End of Apartheid

Alex Cruden and Dedria Bryfonski

Book Editors

GREENHAVEN PRESS
A part of Gale, Cengage Learning

GALE
CENGAGE Learning

Detroit • New York • San Francisco • New Haven, Conn • Waterville, Maine • London

Christine Nasso, *Publisher*
Elizabeth Des Chenes, *Managing Editor*

© 2010 Thomson Gale, a part of Gale, Cengage Learning.

Gale and Greenhaven Press are registered trademarks used herein under license.

For more information, contact:
Greenhaven Press
27500 Drake Rd.
Farmington Hills, MI 48331-3535
Or you can visit our Internet site at gale.cengage.com

For product information and technology assistance, contact us at
Gale Customer Support, 1-800-877-4253.

For permission to use material from this text or product, submit all requests online at
www.cengage.com/permissions.

Further permissions questions can be emailed to permissionrequest@cengage.com

Articles in Greenhaven Press anthologies are often edited for length to meet page requirements. In addition, original titles of these works are changed to clearly present the main thesis and to explicitly indicate the author's opinion. Every effort is made to ensure that Greenhaven Press accurately reflects the original intent of the authors. Every effort has been made to trace the owners of copyrighted material.

Cover image © David Turnley/Corbis

LIBRARY OF CONGRESS CATALOGING-IN-PUBLICATION DATA
The end of apartheid / Alex Cruden and Dedria Bryfonski, book editors.
    p. cm. -- (Perspectives on modern world history)
    Includes bibliographical references and index.
    ISBN 978-0-7377-4557-3 (hardcover)
1. South Africa--Politics and government--20th century--Juvenile literature. 2. Apartheid--Juvenile literature. 3. South Africa--Race relations--Juvenile literature. I. Cruden, Alex. II. Bryfonski, Dedria.
    DT1971.E53 2010
    968.06--dc22
                                             2009027200

Printed in the United States of America
1 2 3 4 5 6 7 13 12 11 10 09

CONTENTS

Representatives of the Organisation of African Unity, after a 1989 meeting in Harare, Zimbabwe, summarize the unjustness of apartheid and set forth guidelines to end it peacefully. The historic declaration becomes the basis for United Nations opposition to apartheid.

states that those who supported sanctions hurt the South Africans they intended to help. Contact with the outside world was more likely to bring change than the isolation that sanctions caused.

apartheid has worn off, and it is clear that the basic tasks of nation-building have been mis-handled by the government.

CHAPTER 3   Personal Narratives

and their expectations, about their pain and their hope.

FOREWORD

"History cannot give us a program for the future, but it can give us a fuller understanding of ourselves, and of our common humanity, so that we can better face the future."
—Robert Penn Warren,
American poet and novelist

The history of each nation is punctuated by momentous events that represent turning points for that nation, with an impact felt far beyond its borders. These events—displaying the full range of human capabilities, from violence, greed, and ignorance to heroism, courage, and strength—are nearly always complicated and multifaceted. Any student of history faces the challenge of grasping the many strands that constitute such world-changing events as wars, social movements, and environmental disasters. But understanding these significant historic events can be enhanced by exposure to a variety of perspectives, whether of people involved intimately or of ones observing from a distance of miles or years. Understanding can also be increased by learning about the controversies surrounding such events and exploring hot-button issues from multiple angles. Finally, true understanding of important historic events involves knowledge of the events' human impact—of the ways such events affected people in their everyday lives—all over the world.

Perspectives on Modern World History examines global historic events from the twentieth-century onward by presenting analysis and observation from numerous vantage points. Each volume offers high school, early college level, and general interest readers a thematically arranged anthology of previously published materials that address a major historical event, with an emphasis on international coverage. Each volume opens with background information on the event, then presents the controversies surrounding that event, and concludes with first-person narratives from people who lived through the event or were affected by it. By providing primary sources from the time of the event, as well as relevant commentary surrounding the event, this series can be used to inform debate, help develop critical thinking skills, increase global awareness, and enhance an understanding of international perspectives on history.

Material in each volume is selected from a diverse range of sources, including journals, magazines, newspapers, nonfiction books, personal narratives, speeches, congressional testimony, government documents, pamphlets, organization newsletters, and position papers. Articles taken from these sources are carefully edited and introduced to provide context and background. Each volume of Perspectives on Modern World History includes an array of views on events of global significance. Much of the material comes from international sources and from U.S. sources that provide extensive international coverage.

Each volume in the Perspectives on Modern World History series also includes:

- A full-color **world map**, offering context and geographic perspective.
- An annotated **table of contents** that provides a brief summary of each essay in the volume.
- An **introduction** specific to the volume topic.
- For each viewpoint, a brief **introduction** that has notes about the author and source of the viewpoint, and that provides a summary of its main points.
- Full-color **charts**, **graphs**, **maps**, and other visual representations.

- Informational **sidebars** that explore the lives of key individuals, give background on historical events, or explain scientific or technical concepts.
- A **glossary** that defines key terms, as needed.
- A **chronology** of important dates preceding, during, and immediately following the event.
- A **bibliography** of additional books, periodicals, and Web sites for further research.
- A comprehensive **subject index** that offers access to people, places, and events cited in the text.

Perspectives on Modern World History is designed for a broad spectrum of readers who want to learn more about not only history but also current events, political science, government, international relations, and sociology—students doing research for class assignments or debates, teachers and faculty seeking to supplement course materials, and others wanting to improve their understanding of history. Each volume of Perspectives on Modern World History is designed to illuminate a complicated event, to spark debate, and to show the human perspective behind the world's most significant happenings of recent decades.

INTRODUCTION

To a degree rare in major historical conflicts, the peaceful ending of apartheid in South Africa was the work of extraordinary individuals, individuals who were in fact part of the conflict. This settlement stands out in world history, amid the centuries of large-scale confrontations primarily decided by war, revolution, mass movement, invasion, intervention by outside agencies, or economic imperatives.

Outside pressure, including economic, was applied to the apartheid-administering government in South Africa, but the effects of the pressure were debatable. What is unquestionable is that certain individuals acted with intelligence, compassion, bravery, insight, and vision—and brought the nation along with them.

On reflection, it is logical that individual action should end apartheid. As a policy, apartheid was all about distinctions between human beings, with a white group of European ancestry declaring itself superior. From its dominant position, the group's leaders restricted nonwhites' education, employment, residence, love life, and movement from place to place. Each individual's rights depended on his or her ancestry and skin color. Apartheid was personal.

The person most responsible for its end was Nelson Mandela, a black man imprisoned for decades for his opposition to the discriminatory white government. Mandela, while behind bars, negotiated the country's way out of apartheid and then later, as the first South African president elected by all the races, led without bitterness or vengeance enacted upon his former oppressors.

An American journalist living in southern Africa, Remer Tyson, wrote that "Mandela will be remembered as a strong-willed African who demanded dignity for himself and his people and got it because he was willing to die—on the gallows or in the loneliness of a prison cell—for democracy. He will be revered as proof that the human spirit can prevail against adversity."

Mandela is one of four South Africans to win the Nobel Peace Prize. Beginning in 1960, more South Africans won the prize than people from anywhere other than the United States, a tribute to both the grave danger apartheid's opponents lived in as well as the profound difficulties of overcoming racial divisions. Even in the long-democratic, free-speech United States, race is the nation's most difficult conversation.

In South Africa, individual positions against apartheid ranged from peaceful efforts within the system to clandestine attacks. Early on, Chief Albert J. Lutuli influentially urged nonviolent progress toward equality. Activist and church leader Desmond Tutu gained worldwide notice with sharply worded yet peace-loving appeals for justice. As a young man, Mandela came to prominence—and punishment—with militant positions. These earned him credibility with a majority of South Africans in his ultimately nonviolent success. And on the white government side, President F.W. de Klerk surprised many supporters by strongly endorsing changes that led to his party's defeat and a predominantly black new administration. These four Nobel winners risked their reputations and lives. The 1984 Nobel declaration honoring Tutu dramatically illustrated the effect—and danger—of standing up individually:

Some time ago television enabled us to see this year's laureate in a suburb of Johannesburg. A massacre of the black population had just taken place—the camera showed ruined houses, mutilated human beings and crushed children's toys. Innocent people had been murdered. Women and children mortally wounded. But, after the police vehicles had driven away with their prisoners, Desmond Tutu stood and spoke to a frightened and bitter congregation: "Do not hate," he said, "let us choose the peaceful way to freedom."

In the face of racism that obviously could kill, racism that stung in every moment of daily life, Tutu's plea to not hate was extraordinary. Yet a multitude of non-white people indeed largely honored Tutu's plea; while they could not banish hate entirely, they did go to great lengths to act peacefully.

It was easier for whites to speak out, though not penalty-free. For years, the most prominent white South African against apartheid was another singular figure, Helen Suzman. Elected to Parliament in 1952, Suzman increasingly spoke up for equality among the races. In 1959 she helped form the Progressive Party, and from 1961 until 1974, when five other party members were elected, she was the only national legislator who fully opposed apartheid. This was at a time when discrimination against women, of any race, also was widespread. Suzman was criticized unmercifully in terms fit for a traitor. Nevertheless, she not only thoroughly questioned and opposed racial oppression measures brought up in Parliament, she traveled to other countries and gave frequent public speeches against apartheid.

This brought her more criticism in Parliament, but the challenges she issued did not abate. On one occasion, a cabinet member shouted, "You put these questions just to embarrass South Africa overseas." Suzman responded: "It is not my questions that embarrass South Africa. It is your answers."

In spite of efforts to peacefully end apartheid, there was some violence throughout the struggle over apartheid. Lethal actions came from many sides. Thousands of people were killed, including the prominent young black activist Steve Biko. Yet, despite the intensity and immensity of the struggle, large-scale warfare did not occur. White and black leaders resolutely progressed toward solutions.

For example, in 1990, when the two main opposing parties—the white-minority government and the predominantly black African National Congress [ANC]—began negotiating who would rule after apartheid, the whites accepted a longtime enemy, Joe Slowo, as part of the ANC team. "It was well that they did so," wrote Robert Ross in *A Concise History of South Africa*, "for this portly, jovial Communist turned out to be not the bogeyman of white fears but rather the most realistic and hard-headed figure on either side."

In another example, Cyril Ramaphosa, a founder and the leader of the National Union of Mineworkers, had been imprisoned by the white government. He had led his largely black union in unsuccessful strikes. He said later: "We were not sophisticated in our approach to negotiations; all we had was just a sense of injustice and a mission to improve the lot of the worker." But, as Patti Waldmeir reported in *Anatomy of a Miracle*, Ramaphosa said he learned "to present our arguments in a clear, articulate and sophisticated way." He went on to be the successful chief negotiator for the ANC in the early 1990s, when South Africa appeared on the brink of tearing itself apart.

Notably, the previously oppressed did not carry out revenge after apartheid was dismantled. Instead, again certain individuals asserted the pre-eminence of humanity. In 1995 Tutu, Alex Boraine, and several other South Africans established the Truth and Reconciliation Commission (TRC), a unique official body that offered healing, closure, and amnesty in place of scarring, blame, and punishment. The TRC made its decisions case by case, person by person. The emphasis was on individuality rather than on mass or abstract conceptualizations. Subsequently, when the African National Congress became the major party in the new government, it sustained the TRC's dedication to peaceful measures.

As the viewpoints in *Perspectives on Modern World History: The End of Apartheid* show, while certain large-scale actions helped in the struggle against apartheid, heroic individuals broke its chains.

World Map

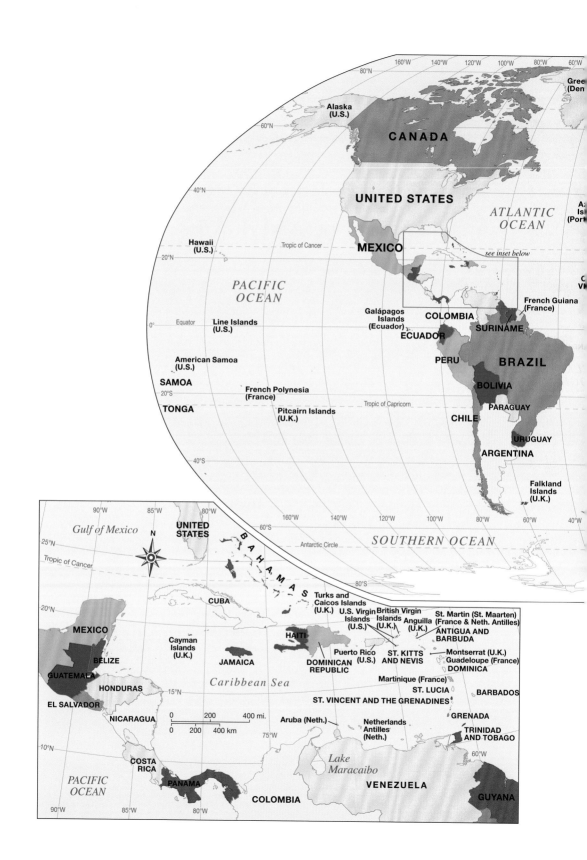

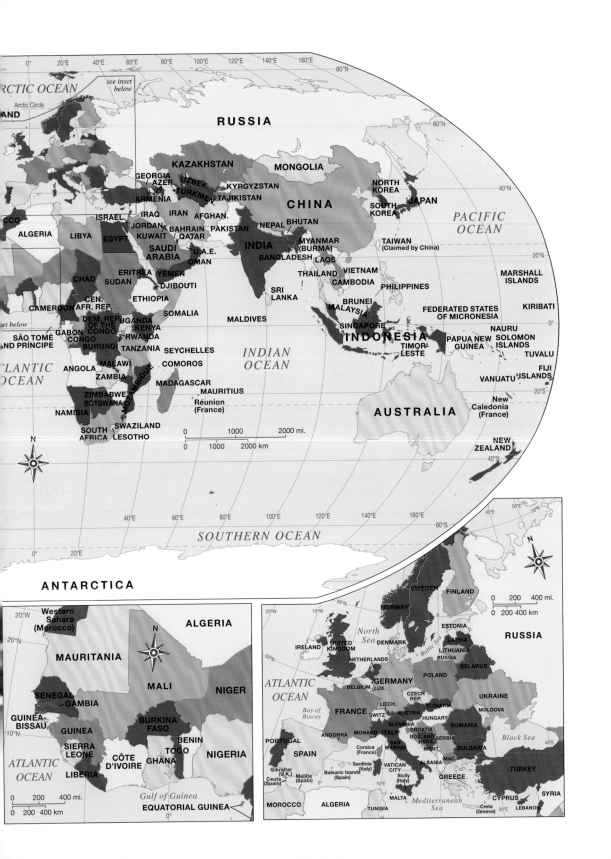

CHAPTER 1

Historical Background on the End of Apartheid

White Privilege Established Domination for Forty-Five Years

Betty J. Harris

In the following selection, Betty J. Harris explains how racial subjugation in South Africa began centuries ago but reached a peak of legalization in the twentieth century. Dutch-ancestry white people known as Afrikaners dominated the government and society with a system called apartheid, which preserved their privileges even though they were a small minority of the country's population. Black opposition grew in the 1980s and eventually succeeded in ending apartheid. Author and professor Betty J. Harris has taught at several U.S. universities.

Photo on previous page: Protesters flee riot-control police, who break up a 1985 antiapartheid demonstration in South Africa. (William F. Campbell/Time Life Pictures/Getty Images.)

*A*partheid, an Afrikaans word meaning "apartness," describes an ideology of racial segregation that served as the basis for white domination of the

---

SOURCE. Betty J. Harris, *New Dictionary of the History of Ideas.* Belmont, CA: Charles Scribner's Sons, 2005. Copyright © 2005 Gale, Cengage Learning. Reproduced by permission of Gale, a part of Cengage Learning.

South African state from 1948 to 1994. Apartheid represented the codification of the racial segregation that had been practiced in South Africa from the time of the Cape Colony's founding by the Dutch East India Company in 1652. . . . Widely perceived internationally as one of the most abhorrent human rights issues from the 1970s to the 1990s, apartheid conjured up images of white privilege and black marginalization implemented by a police state that strictly enforced black subordination.

> "Afrikaners viewed their history in terms of a repeating suffering-and-death cycle at the hands of the British."

Historical Background

The Dutch East India Company occupied the Cape Colony uninterruptedly from 1652 until the British takeover in 1795. The company's conflict with the indigenous Khoisan was exacerbated by its granting of farmland to company members who had completed their term of service. The Khoisan, who became indentured servants, were landless by the time of the British occupation. Slaves were imported from Asia and elsewhere in Africa throughout the eighteenth century. Briefly restored to Dutch rule in 1803, the colony was again brought under British control in 1806. Two events to which Dutch settlers reacted negatively were the British abolition of the slave trade in 1806 and of slavery in 1833. The latter precipitated the Great Trek, in which many Dutch (Afrikaner) farmers migrated outside the Cape Colony.

A "mineral revolution," financed by British capital, began in South Africa with the discovery of diamonds in Kimberley in 1868 and gold in Johannesburg in 1886. Later the British victory [over the Afrikaners] in the Boer War (1899–1902) brought the Transvaal and the Orange Free State [colonies] under British rule. Natal was already a British colony. Collectively the four colonies formed the Union of South Africa in 1910.

Afrikaners, who suffered military defeat in the war, displayed intense anti-British sentiment as many of their farms were destroyed and their wives and children placed in concentration camps, resulting in a high mortality rate. Their efforts to increase their population contributed to proletarianization, precipitating their migration to cities for employment. They often became squatters alongside poor blacks. In 1928–1932 the Carnegie Corporation conducted a study of the "poor white problem" and made recommendations for improving the status of working-class Afrikaners. During that period, Afrikaans, a Dutch variant, became a written language. Members of the emerging Afrikaner bourgeoisie opened the first Afrikaner bank and insurance company.

The Rise of Afrikaner Nationalism

After the Boer War, two Afrikaner generals, Jan Smuts and Louis Botha, sought conciliation with the British in forming the South African Party. Supporters also included enfranchised blacks. The South African Party defeated the Unionist Party in the 1910 elections. Cognizant of eroding political rights, members of the black educated elite formed the South African Native National Congress (later the African National Congress [ANC]) in 1912. Racist legislation enacted during this period of "fusion" included the 1913 Land Act, which prohibited a type of sharecropping called farming-on-the-half, in which black sharecroppers negotiated with white farmers to farm part of the latter's land. Furthermore, blacks could not own land outside of designated areas.

Another Afrikaner general, J.B.M. Hertzog, led dissidents against a South African alliance with the British in World War I. A schism developed between Smuts and Hertzog over South African involvement in World War II, signaling the end of fusion. It was then that Hertzog advocated a South African republic outside the British Commonwealth. Further racist legislation included:

- The Urban Areas Act of 1923, which legislated urban racial segregation, discouraging blacks from becoming town-rooted.

- The Industrial Reconciliation Act of 1926, which introduced job protections for poor whites.

- The 1936 Land Act, which reinforced the 1913 Land Act and designated homelands as areas for African land ownership.

- A 1936 decree that struck Africans in the Cape Province from the common voters' roll.

The historian T. Dunbar Moodie has suggested that Afrikaner nationalism was a civil religion representing the integration of key symbolic elements. These include major events in Afrikaner history, the Afrikaans language, and Dutch Calvinism. From Moodie's perspective, Afrikaners viewed their history in terms of a repeating suffering-and-death cycle at the hands of the British through major events such as the Great Trek and the Boer War. The Broederbond, a secret society composed of Afrikaner professionals, formed the Federation of Afrikaner Cultural Organizations (FAK), affiliating cultural and language associations as well as church councils, youth groups, and scientific study circles in 1929.

Black Resistance

Black activism increased after World War II in South Africa as elsewhere in Africa. When A.B. Xuma became president-general of the African National Congress (ANC) in 1940, he attempted to unify the organization ideologically, regulate its finances, and conduct a propaganda campaign. A major schism developed when Xuma and a few middle-class members advocated negotiation through African representative bodies, while more militant members leaned toward the Communist Party and more assertive political activism.

In the mid-1940s a group of young professionals, including Nelson Mandela and Robert Sobukwe, banded together to form the ANC Youth League. They made overtures to Coloured and Indian political organizations in their call for majority rule. Coloureds were descendants of "miscegenation" [mixture of races] that occurred in the Cape after the Dutch East India Company's occupation. Indians were recruited as indentured servants to work on Natal's sugar plantations in the 1860s.

> "The Ministry of Native Affairs planned a curriculum to prepare the 'Bantu' (South African blacks) to occupy a servile position in South African society."

Apartheid Legislation

After the National Party victory in 1948, a battery of laws was enacted to strictly segregate South African society by race, ethnicity, and class. The Prohibition of Mixed Marriages Act of 1949 outlawed marriages between whites and blacks. The Population Registration Act of 1950 required that each adult South African be classified by ethnic group as follows: white (Afrikaners and English), Coloured (mixed race, Asian [mostly Indian]), and African (Xhosa, Zulu, Ndebele, Swazi, Basotho, Batswana, Bapedi, Venda, and Tsonga). In 1951 South Africa's "African" population was approximately 8.5 million, nearly four-fifths of the entire population. . . .

The Suppression of Communism Act of 1950 forced the disbandment of the South African Communist Party and a diplomatic break with the Soviet Union. The Bantu Authorities Act of 1951 abolished the Natives Representative Council, replacing it with indirect rule. The Natives (Abolition of Passes and Coordination of Documents) Act of 1952 required the assignment of detailed reference books to all pass holders detailing their background, employment, and residential rights outside the reserves.

SOUTH AFRICAN HOMELANDS UNDER APARTHEID

Ghanzi

Windhoek ★   Gobabis

NAMIBIA   BOTSWANA

Keetmanshoop

BOPHUTHATSWANA

Hotazel

Upington

Kimberley

CAPE

SOUTH
ATLANTIC
OCEAN

SOUTH AFRICA

Beaufort West

Saldanha

Cape Town

Mosselbaai

Taken from: *New Dictionary of History of Ideas*, Charles Scribner's Sons.

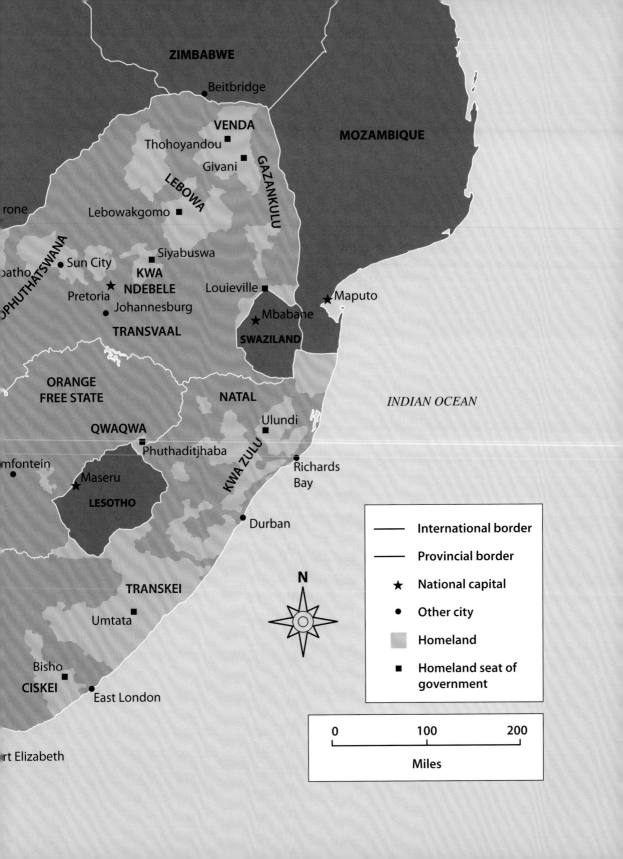

Parliament also passed the Bantu Education Act of 1953, providing for state control of African schools, which had mostly been founded by missionary societies, at the primary, secondary, and tertiary levels. The Ministry of Native Affairs planned a curriculum to prepare the "Bantu" (South African blacks) to occupy a servile position in South African society. Undocumented Africans were removed from urban areas to rural homelands under the provisions of the Native Resettlement Act of 1954. Cape Coloureds were removed from the common voters' roll in the Cape Province in 1956.

When Hendrik F. Verwoerd, minister of native affairs from 1950, became prime minister in 1958, he continued to initiate apartheid legislation compatible with his views regarding "separate development." The Promotion of Bantu Self-Government Act of 1959 provided for the creation of eight national units for African self-government supposedly reflective of African ethnic groupings. Since urban blacks had no political representation, it devolved upon chiefs to act as roving ambassadors between African subjects in the urban areas and those resident in homelands. Homelands or reserve areas represented 13.7 percent of the land.

The Bantu Homelands Act of 1970 required that all Africans be given exclusive citizenship in a homeland, disregarding place of birth and current residence. In 1972 Zululand and Bophuthatswana were granted self-governing status, while Transkei, self-governing since 1963, was given more autonomy as the model homeland. Transkei's "independence" in 1976 was followed by Bophuthatswana in 1977, Venda in 1979, and Ciskei in 1981.

The Western Cape was declared a Coloured labor preference area in the 1950s. Indians, granted citizenship in 1963, experienced racial discrimination in residential and trading rights.

Two Kinds of Whites

White people ran the government of what became the nation of South Africa for centuries. But they were not always united. In fact, at one point they were at war.

In African terms, there were two white tribes. One began as predominantly Dutch, starting with traders and explorers who founded the southern city of Cape Town in the 1650s. They were later known as Boers and as Afrikaners. This group reached a peak of power in creating the apartheid government in 1948 and administering it.

The other white group was mainly British. They gained a foothold of power in 1806, when they took over the Cape Town area. Many Boers then headed north and established their own territorial governments.

During 1899–1902, the two sides fought what is known as the Boer War, primarily over gold, diamonds and power. The British won, but the rivalry continued. In general, the English concentrated on economic dominance and the Afrikaners on government control. Each side maintained its own language—English and Afrikaans.

The two groups did collaborate in one respect: maintaining white dominance of the country, even though combined they made up only a small fraction of the total population.

Gender Issues

Helen Suzman, a long-term antiapartheid member of parliament (MP), observed that in 1953, her first year, there were actually four women in parliament. Two were fellow United Party members, and one was a member of the Liberal Party. Suzman, a liberal, dealt primarily with racial issues, although she also advocated equal rights for women regarding marriage, divorce, abortion, and employment. White women had been enfranchised in 1930 to counter the nonwhite male vote. In general racial and gender issues were not intertwined. However, in 1955 liberal white women founded the Black Sash to protest the proposed disenfranchisement of Coloured men.

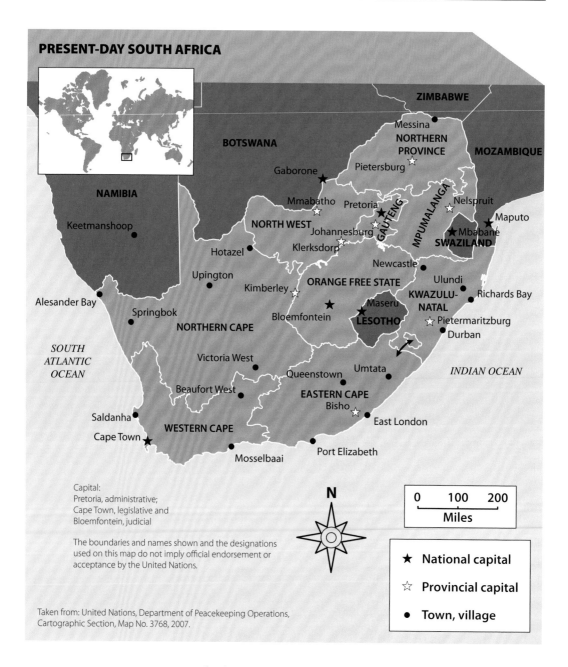

PRESENT-DAY SOUTH AFRICA

Capital:
Pretoria, administrative;
Cape Town, legislative and
Bloemfontein, judicial

The boundaries and names shown and the designations
used on this map do not imply official endorsement or
acceptance by the United Nations.

Taken from: United Nations, Department of Peacekeeping Operations,
Cartographic Section, Map No. 3768, 2007.

★ National capital

☆ Provincial capital

● Town, village

Black women were particularly discriminated against
with influx control and pass laws, extended to women in
1956. Influx control was a policy designed to direct the
flow of black labor to "white" urban areas for employ-

ment and to rural farms. With the Nationalist victory in 1948, influx control regulations were enhanced. Pass laws regulated document requirements for black people. Jacklyn Cock examined their status as domestic servants in suburban white households. In *Maids and Madams*, Cock reports on a study of 800,000 black

> "Students in the Johannesburg township rioted when the government made Afrikaans the language of school instruction in science subjects."

domestic servants. She examines their status as workers and mothers and their dependency relationships with their white madams. Black domestic workers neglected their own families to be at the beck and call of the white madams and often lived in servants' quarters near the madams' houses. This enabled the madam to engage in leisure activities or to pursue employment to enhance her family's income. Cock illuminates gradations of female exploitation in the South African context in focusing on the relationship between maid and madam.

Increasing Black Nationalism

In 1952 the African National Congress, whose membership was estimated at 100,000, organized a campaign of defiance to protest racially discriminatory laws, burning passes and defying regulations concerning segregated facilities. Eighty-five hundred people were arrested during the four-month campaign, which resulted in a treason trial and the eventual acquittal of the accused. In 1955 the African National Congress and similar political organizations met and drafted the Freedom Charter, which embraced the tenets of a nonracial, democratic society in which major capitalist enterprises would be nationalized.

Ideological differences within the ANC resulted in Robert Sobukwe breaking away to form the Pan-Africanist Congress (PAC) in 1959. In 1960 the PAC organized a campaign to protest pass laws and low wages.

After publicly burning their government-issued passbooks to protest apartheid, Black South Africans queue to receive new papers, which are required for individuals to be able to work. (AP Images.)

At Sharpeville, near Johannesburg, in March 1960, police opened fire on a crowd of demonstrators, killing 69 and injuring some 180. The government declared a state of emergency and arrested 1,600 people. The massacre precipitated international condemnation of the South African government, diminished investor confidence, and threw the economy into recession.

After Sharpeville, the ANC and PAC were banned, initiating underground political activity. Nelson Mandela, who had already been imprisoned on other charges, and his compatriots, taken into custody at a farm in the Johannesburg suburb of Rivonia, site of the ANC's underground headquarters, were charged with sabotage and conspiracy to overthrow the government. In 1964 all but one of the codefendants were sentenced to life imprisonment. The Rivonia trial signaled the cessation of black nationalist resistance in South Africa. Many members of banned organizations sought refuge in other countries. Neighboring colonies provided South Africa a protective buffer against guerrilla insurgency, investor confidence was restored, and the country embarked on a period of economic prosperity. Meanwhile, after an all-white referendum, South Africa was declared a republic outside the commonwealth in 1961.

Dismantling of Apartheid

The outbreak of the Soweto riots in 1976 marked the denouement in the South African struggle. Students in the Johannesburg township rioted when the government made Afrikaans the language of school instruction in science subjects. Combating police bullets with sticks and stones, hundreds of students were killed. Others fled the country. The ANC set up recruitment stations in Mozambique from which refugees were transferred for military training. Coloured students in Cape Town intensified their activism. Unrest continued around the country and lasted well into 1977, having a deleterious effect on the economy. Refugees, both male and female, began to infiltrate the country to conduct acts of sabotage.

South Africa's protective buffers began to erode in 1975 with the independence of Angola and Mozambique, followed by that of Zimbabwe in 1980, allowing for increasing guerrilla infiltration into the country. After the Muldergate information scandal, P.W. Botha, minister of defense, became prime minister in 1978. Muldergate was an information scandal in which substantial sums of money allocated to buy international media support for apartheid was funneled to the *Citizen*, a pro-government newspaper in Johannesburg. The disclosure and attempted cover-up precipitated dissension within the ranks of the National Party. Botha's total strategy combined militarism and reform.

Recognizing the potential for a racial bloodbath, the Nationalists sought a "consociational democracy" in which no racial group would dominate. In an effort to bring legitimate leaders to the negotiating table, a campaign began to free the long-imprisoned ANC leader Nelson Mandela in the early 1980s. The president (formerly prime minister) proposed a tricameral parliament with chambers for Asians, Coloureds, and whites. The exclusion of those classified African led to the formation of the United Democratic Front to coordinate activism within the country.

In the mid-1980s major Western powers initiated economic sanctions against apartheid South Africa. Governmental negotiations began in 1990, when Mandela was released from prison. The ANC and other liberation organizations were "unbanned," or legitimized. An interim constitution was written, and elections were held in 1994. The ANC was victorious nationally.

Apartheid Laws Covered Almost Every Aspect of Life

Rita M. Byrnes

In this excerpt from a Library of Congress series on various countries, editor Rita M. Byrnes summarizes the major measures that turned white supremacy into the law of the land in South Africa. The apartheid restrictions on nonwhites' lives— including where they could live and work, whom they could marry, and for whom they could vote—lasted four decades. Rita M. Byrnes is an Africa specialist for the Federal Research Division of the Library of Congress.

[A]fter the 1948 election, President Daniel F.] Malan and the National Party, fearing that they might lose office in the next election, immediately set about introducing laws to give apartheid a legislative reality that could not easily be overturned.

SOURCE. Rita M. Byrnes, *South Africa: A Country Study.* Government Printing Office for the Library of Congress, 1996.

Such laws aimed at separating whites and blacks, at instituting as a legal principle the theory that whites should be treated more favorably than blacks and that separate facilities need not be equal, and at providing the state with the powers deemed necessary to deal with any opposition.

New Laws Divide the Races

The Population Registration Act of 1950 provided the basis for separating the population of South Africa into different races. Under the terms of this act, all residents of South Africa were to be classified as white, coloured, or native (later called Bantu) people. Indians . . . were included under the category "Asian" in 1959. The act required that people be classified primarily on the basis of their "community acceptability"; later amendments placed greater stress on "appearance" in order to deal with the practice of light-colored blacks "passing" as whites. The act also provided for the compilation of a population register for the whole country and for the issuing of identity cards.

Other laws provided for geographic, social, and political separation. The Group Areas Act of 1950 extended the provisions of the Natives Land Act of 1913; and later laws divided South Africa into separate areas for whites and blacks (including coloureds [people of mixed race]), and gave the government the power to forcibly remove people from areas not designated for their particular racial group. The Tomlinson Commission in 1954 officially concluded that the areas set aside for Africans would support no more than two-thirds of the African population even under the best of conditions, but the government ignored its recommendation that more land be allocated to the reserves and began removing Africans from white areas.

The Prohibition of Mixed Marriages Act of 1949 made marriages between whites and members of other racial groups illegal. The Immorality Act of 1950 extended an earlier ban on sexual relations between whites and blacks (the Immorality Act of 1927) to a ban on sexual relations between whites and any non-whites. The Bantu Authorities Act of 1951 established Bantu tribal, regional, and territorial authorities in the regions set out for Africans under the Group Areas Act, and it abolished the Natives Representative Council. The Bantu authorities were to be dominated by chiefs and headmen appointed by the government. The government also sought in 1951 to remove coloured voters in the Cape from the common roll onto a separate roll and to require that they elect white representatives only (Separate Representation of Voters Act of 1951). The Supreme Court immediately declared the act invalid on constitutional grounds,

A sign in apartheid-era South Africa restricts a bayside beach to whites only. (**AP Images**.)

but after a long struggle it was successfully reenacted (the Separate Representation of Voters Amendment Act of 1956).

Laws Make Education and Jobs Worse for Nonwhites

The concept of unequal allocation of resources was built into legislation on general facilities, education, and jobs. The Reservation of Separate Amenities Act of 1953 stated that all races should have separate amenities—such as toilets, parks, and beaches—and that these need not be of an equivalent quality. Under the provisions of this act, apartheid signs were erected throughout South Africa.

The Bantu Education Act of 1953 decreed that blacks should be provided with separate educational facilities under the control of the Ministry of Native Affairs, rather than the Ministry of Education. The pupils in these schools would be taught their Bantu cultural heritage and, in the words of Hendrik F. Verwoerd, minister of native affairs, would be trained "in accordance with their opportunities in life," which he considered did not reach "above the level of certain forms of labour." The act also removed state subsidies from denominational schools with the result that most of the mission-run African institutions (with the exception of some schools run by the Roman Catholic Church and the Seventh Day Adventists) were sold to the government or closed. The Extension of University Education Act of 1959 prohibited blacks from attending white institutions, with few exceptions, and established separate universities and colleges for Africans, coloureds, and Indians.

The Industrial Conciliation Act of 1956 enabled the minister of labour to reserve categories of work for members of specified

> Neither men nor women could remain in an urban area for longer than seventy-two hours without a special permit stating that they were legally employed.

In Between Black and White

Apartheid formalized a distinction within non-white peoples: there were blacks and there were coloreds. Colored people included those of mixed race and those whose families came from India and elsewhere in Asia. Any child of a white parent and a nonwhite parent was designated as colored.

The apartheid government classified people as colored based on how they looked as well as on their ancestry.

The main law dividing the country's people into white, colored and black was the 1950 Population Registration Act.

Under apartheid, colored people had slightly better official rights than black people did. Some apartheid critics called the distinction diabolically clever because it created rivalries among the non-white peoples and meant colored people had something to lose if they allied with blacks.

Not all statistics and related characterizations of South African history use the same demographic distinctions. Sometimes the categories are simply black and white, with colored people counted as black. In some instances, "colored" is divided into two categories, mixed-race and Asian.

racial groups. In effect, if the minister felt that white workers were being pressured by "unfair competition" from blacks, he could recategorize jobs for whites only and increase their rates of pay. Under the terms of the Native Laws Amendment Act of 1952, African women as well as men were made subject to influx control and the pass laws [laws segregating the population and restricting their movements] and, under Section 10 of the act, neither men nor women could remain in an urban area for longer than seventy-two hours without a special permit stating that they were legally employed. The Abolition of Passes and Co-ordination of Documents Act of 1952, which was designed to make the policy of pass restrictions easier, abolished the pass, replacing it with a document known as a "reference book." The act stated that all Africans had to carry a reference book containing their photograph, address, marital status, employment record, list of taxes paid, influx control endorsements, and rural district where officially resident; not having the reference book on one's person was a criminal offense punishable by a prison sentence.

> The Native Administration Act of 1956 permitted the government to 'banish' Africans, essentially exiling them to remote rural areas far from their homes.

The White Government Insists on Order

Whereas the above laws built largely on existing legislation, police powers underwent a much greater expansion. The Suppression of Communism Act of 1950 had declared the Communist Party and its ideology illegal. Among other features, the act defined communism as any scheme that aimed "at bringing about any political, industrial, social, or economic change within the Union by the promotion of disturbance or disorder" or that encouraged "feelings of hostility between the European and the non-European races of the Union the consequences of which are calculated to further . . ." disorder. The act allowed the minister of justice to list members of such organizations and to ban them, usually for five-year periods, from public office, from attending public meetings, or from being in any specified area of South Africa. The Public Safety Act of 1953 gave the British governor general power to suspend all laws and to proclaim a state of emergency. The Criminal Law Amendment Act of 1953 stated that anyone accompanying a person found guilty of offenses committed while "protest[ing], or in support of any campaign for the repeal or modification of any law," would also be presumed guilty and would have the burden of proving his or her innocence. The Native Administration Act of 1956 permitted the government to "banish" Africans, essentially exiling them to remote rural areas far from their homes. The Customs and Excise Act of 1955 and the Official Secrets Act of 1956 gave the government power to establish a Board of Censors to censor books, films, and other materials imported into or produced in South Africa. During the 1950s, enforcement of these various laws resulted in approximately 500,000 pass-law arrests annually, in the listing of more than 600 inhabitants as communists, in the banning of nearly 350 inhabitants, and in the banishment of more than 150 other inhabitants.

African Nations Unite on a Plan to End Apartheid

Ad Hoc Committee on Southern Africa of the Organisation of African Unity

A 1989 meeting of the Organisation of African Unity (OAU) in Harare, the capital of Zimbabwe, just north of South Africa, produced a statement setting forth the case against apartheid. This declaration, which became profoundly influential, describes apartheid as a crime against humanity. The declaration affirms the importance of South Africa becoming a just and democratic nation, a change that would benefit that nation and all the countries in the region.

The Organisation of African Unity was founded in 1963 to promote cooperation and development among all African nations. The OAU sought to eradicate colonialism and played a major role in bringing about the end of apartheid in South Africa.

SOURCE. The Ad Hoc Committee on Southern Africa of the Organisation of African Unity, "Harare Declaration, Declaration of the OAU Ad-hoc Committee on Southern Africa on the Question of South Africa, Harare, Zimbabwe," *African National Congress*, August 21, 1989. Reproduced by permission.

The Ad Hoc Committee on Southern Africa of the Organisation of African Unity [OAU]—consisting of several Heads of State—adopted a Declaration at its meeting in Harare in August 1989, at the suggestion of the African National Congress, recognising that "a conjuncture of circumstances exists which, if there is a demonstrable readiness on the part of the Pretoria regime to engage in negotiations genuinely and sincerely, could create the possibility to end apartheid through negotiations". It then laid down a statement of principles and modalities for negotiations.

The Declaration was endorsed by the Movement of Non-aligned States at its summit meeting in Belgrade, and formed the basis for the "Declaration on Apartheid and its Destructive Consequences in Southern Africa" adopted by the United Nations General Assembly on 14 December 1989.

Preamble

1. The people of Africa, singly, collectively and acting through the OAU, are engaged in serious efforts to establish peace throughout the continent by ending all conflicts through negotiations based on the principle of justice and peace for all.

2. We reaffirm our conviction, which history confirms, that where colonial, racial and apartheid domination exists, there can neither be peace nor justice.

3. Accordingly, we reiterate that while the apartheid system in South Africa persists, the peoples of our continent as a whole cannot achieve the fundamental objectives of justice, human dignity and peace which are both crucial in themselves and fundamental to the stability and development of Africa.

4. With regard to the region of Southern Africa, the entire continent is vitally interested that the processes, in which it is involved, leading to the com-

> The Pretoria regime must abandon its abhorrent concepts and practices of racial domination.

plete and genuine independence of Namibia, as well as peace in Angola and Mozambique, should succeed in the shortest possible time. Equally, Africa is deeply concerned that the destabilisation by South Africa of all the countries of the region, whether through direct aggression, sponsorship of surrogates, economic subversion and other means, should end immediately.

5. We recognise the reality that permanent peace and stability in Southern Africa can only be achieved when the system of apartheid in South Africa has been liquidated and South Africa transformed into a united, democratic and non-racial country. We therefore reiterate that all the necessary measures should be adopted now, to bring a speedy end to the apartheid system, in the interest of all the people of Southern Africa, our continent and the world at large.

6. We believe that, as a result of the liberation struggle and international pressure against apartheid, as well as global efforts to liquidate regional conflicts, possibilities exist for further movement towards the resolution of the problems facing the people of South Africa. For these possibilities to lead to fundamental change in South Africa, the Pretoria regime must abandon its abhorrent concepts and practices of racial domination and its record of failure to honour agreements all of which have already resulted in the loss of lives and the destruction of much property in the countries of Southern Africa.

7. We reaffirm our recognition of the rights of all peoples, including those of South Africa, to determine their own destiny, and to work out for themselves the institutions and the system of government

under which they will, by general consent, live and work together to build a harmonious society. The Organisation of African Unity remains committed to do everything possible and necessary, to assist the people of South Africa, in such ways as the representatives of the oppressed may determine, to achieve this objective. We are certain that, arising from this duty to help end the criminal apartheid system, the rest of the world community is ready to extend similar assistance to the people of South Africa.

8. We make these commitments because we believe that all people are equal and have equal rights to human dignity and respect, regardless of colour, race, sex or creed. We believe that all men and women have the right and duty to participate in their own government, as equal members of society. No individual or group of individuals has any rights to govern others without their consent. The apartheid system violates all these fundamental and universal principles. Correctly characterised as a crime against humanity, it is responsible for the death of countless numbers of people in South Africa, resulting in untold loss of life, destruction of property and massive displacement of innocent men, women and children. This scourge and affront to humanity must be fought and eradicated in its totality.

> We . . . support all those in South Africa who pursue this noble objective [of ending apartheid] through political, armed and other forms of struggle.

9. We have therefore supported and continue to support all those in South Africa who pursue this noble objective through political, armed and other forms of struggle. We believe this to be our duty, carried out in the interest of all humanity.

10. While extending this support to those who strive for a non-racial and democratic society in South Africa, a point on which no compromise is possible, we have repeatedly expressed our preference for a solution arrived at by peaceful means. We know that the majority of the people of South Africa and their liberation movement, who have been compelled to take up arms, have also upheld this position for many decades and continue to do so.

11. The positions contained in this Declaration are consistent with and are a continuation of those elaborated in the Lusaka Manifesto, two decades ago. They take into account the changes that have taken place in South Africa since that Manifesto was adopted by the OAU and the rest of the international community. They constitute a new challenge to the Pretoria regime to join in the noble effort to end the apartheid system, an objective to which the OAU has been committed from its birth.

> There shall be created an economic order which shall promote and advance the well-being of all South Africans.

12. Consequently, we shall continue to do everything in our power to help intensify the liberation struggle and international pressure against the system of apartheid until this system is ended and South Africa is transformed into a united democratic and non-racial country, with justice and security for all its citizens.

13. In keeping with this solemn resolve, and responding to the wishes of the representatives of the majority of the people of South Africa, we publically pledge ourselves to the positions contained hereunder. We are convinced that their implementation will lead to the speedy end of the apartheid system and therefore the opening of a new dawn of peace for all the

peoples of Africa, in which racism, colonial domination and white minority rule on our continent would be abolished for ever.

Statement of Principles

14. We believe that a conjuncture of circumstances exists which, if there is a demonstrable readiness on the part of the Pretoria regime to engage in negotiations genuinely and seriously, could create the possibility to end apartheid through negotiations. Such an eventuality would be an expression of the long-standing preference of the people of South Africa to arrive at a political settlement.

15. We would therefore encourage the people of South Africa, as part of their overall struggle, to get together to negotiate an end to the apartheid system and agree on all the measures that are necessary to transform their country into a non-racial democracy. We support the position held by the majority of the people of South Africa that these objectives and not the amendment or reform of the apartheid system, should be the aims of the negotiations.

16. We are at one with them that the outcome of such a process should be a new constitutional order based on the following principles, among others:

    16.1. South Africa shall become a united, democratic and non-racial state.

    16.2. All its people shall enjoy common and equal citizenship and nationality, regardless of race, colour, sex or creed.

    16.3. All its people shall have the right to participate in the government and administration of the country on the basis of a universal suffrage, exercised through one person one vote, under a common voters roll.

16.4. All people have the right to form and join any political party of their choice, provided that this is not in the furtherance of racism.

16.5. All shall enjoy universally recognised human rights, freedoms and civil liberties, protected under an entrenched Bill of Rights.

16.6. South Africa shall have a new legal system which shall guarantee equality of all before the law.

16.7. South Africa shall have an independent and non-racial judiciary.

16.8. There shall be created an economic order which shall promote and advance the well-being of all South Africans.

16.9. A democratic South Africa shall respect the rights and sovereignty and territorial integrity of all countries and pursue a policy of peace, friendship and mutually beneficial co-operation with all people.

17. We believe that the agreement on the principles shall continue the foundation for an internationally acceptable solution which shall enable South Africa to take its rightful place as an equal partner among the African and world community of nations.

Climate for Negotiations

18. Together with the rest of the world, we believe that it is essential, before any negotiations take place, that the necessary climate for negotiations be created. The apartheid regime has the urgent responsibility to respond positively to this universally acclaimed demand and thus create this climate.

19. Accordingly, the present regime should, at the very least:

Photo on previous page: Approximately 10,000 protesters who marched at a Johannesburg police headquarters on September 15, 1989. Numerous activists were detained and interrogated. (AP Images.)

19.1. Release all political prisoners and detainees unconditionally and refrain from imposing any restrictions on them.

19.2. Lift all bans and restrictions on all proscribed and restricted organisations and people.

19.3. Remove all troops from the townships.

19.4. End the state of emergency and repeal all legislation, such as, and including, the Internal Security Act, designed to circumscribe political activity.

19.5. Cease all political executions.

20. These measures are necessary to produce the conditions in which free discussion can take place—an essential condition to ensure that the people themselves participate in the process of remaking their country. The measures listed above should therefore precede negotiations.

Guidelines to the Process of Negotiation

21. We support the view of the South African liberation movement that upon the creation of this climate, the process of negotiations should commence along the following lines:

21.1. Discussions should take place between the liberation movement and the South African regime to achieve the suspension of hostilities on both sides by agreeing to a mutually binding cease fire.

21.2. Negotiations should then proceed to establish the basis for the adoption of a new Constitution by agreeing on, among others, the Principles enunciated above.

21.3. Having agreed on these Principles, the parties

should then negotiate the necessary mecha-
nism for drawing up the new Constitution.

21.4. The parties shall define and agree on the
role to be played by the
international community
in ensuring a successful
transition to a democratic
order.

> We appeal to all people of good-
> will throughout the world to sup-
> port this Programme of Action.

21.5. The parties shall agree on
the formation of an interim
government to supervise
the process of the drawing up and adoption
of a new constitution; govern and administer
the country, as well as effect the transition to a
democratic order including the holding of the
elections.

21.6. After the adoption of the new Constitution, all
armed hostilities will be deemed to have for-
mally terminated.

21.7. For its part, the international community would lift the sanctions that have been
imposed against apartheid South Africa.

22. The new South Africa shall qualify for the membership of the Organisation of African Unity.

Programme of Action

23. In pursuance of the objectives stated in this document, Organisation of African Unity hereby com-
mits itself to:

23.1. Inform governments and inter-governmental
organisations throughout the world, including the Non-Aligned Movement, the United
Nations General Assembly, the Security
Council, the Commonwealth and others of
these perspectives, and solicit their support.

23.2. Mandate the OAU ad-hoc committee on Southern Africa, acting as the representative of the OAU, assisted by the Frontline States [the nations bordering South Africa] to remain seized of the issue of a political resolution to the South Africa question.

23.3. Step up all-round support for the South African liberation movement and campaign in the rest of the world in pursuance of this objective.

23.4. Intensify the campaign for mandatory and comprehensive sanctions against apartheid South Africa; in this regard, immediately mobilise against the re-scheduling of Pretoria's foreign debts; work for the imposition of a mandatory oil embargo and the full observance by all countries of the arms embargo.

23.5. Ensure that the African continent does not relax existing measures for the total isolation of apartheid South Africa.

23.6. Continue to monitor the situation in Namibia and extend all necessary support to SWAPO in its struggle for a genuinely independent Namibia.

23.7. Extend such assistance as the Governments of Angola and Mozambique may request in order to secure peace for their people.

23.8. Render all possible assistance to the Frontline States to enable them to withstand Pretoria's campaign of aggression and destabilisation and enable them to continue to give their all-round support to the people of Namibia and South Africa.

24. We appeal to all people of goodwill throughout the world to support this Programme of Action as a

necessary measure to secure the earliest liquidation of the apartheid system and the transformation of South Africa into a united, democratic and non-racial country.

The Afrikaner Leader Moves Toward Security and Justice for All

F.W. de Klerk

In this excerpt from the South African equivalent of a State of the Union address, F.W. de Klerk, the South African president, states the importance of South Africa making the transition to a representational democracy. He calls for an end to political violence and for the establishment of a bill of rights for all South Africans. The speech came two years before the first multiracial national election, the one that chose Nelson Mandela as de Klerk's successor.

F.W. de Klerk was first elected to Parliament in 1972 and became South Africa's president in 1989.

SOURCE. F.W. de Klerk, "Address by State President FW de Klerk DMS at the Opening of the Fourth Session of the Ninth Parliament of the Republic of South Africa," *FW de Klerk Foundation*, January 24, 1992. Reproduced by permission.

S outh Africa is looking back today on two years of unprecedented and dynamic change. It is noticeable and tangible in every sphere of life. Nothing and nobody has been left untouched by it. Everywhere it has finally dawned upon everybody that we are experiencing a decisive period in our history.

Out of this era will be born a new constitutional order. It will differ incisively from the present dispensation. To that all South Africans now have to reconcile themselves once and for all. Without it, lasting peace cannot be achieved. For it the Government has obtained a mandate which it will implement responsibly and constitutionally. . . .

We are . . . firmly on course towards our goal of a free and democratic constitutional system based on the principle of representation for all and the elimination of domination and abuse of power. . . .

A National Vote Including All Races

We are honour-bound to hold a referendum which will offer the electorates of each of the three Houses of Parliament the opportunity to express themselves on any substantive changes to the Constitution that may be proposed. At the same time, we also believe that the section of our population that does not take part in Parliamentary elections at present, that is our Black population, should also be given the opportunity of expressing itself in such a referendum.

Therefore, I envisage a referendum in which every South African will be able to take part and in which the result may be determined globally as well as per Parliamentary voters' rolls. In this way, the legitimacy of any transitional Government will be placed beyond doubt in a democratic manner. . . .

> " There is suspicion that the Government's proposal concerning transitional government is designed to ensure continued domination by Whites. "

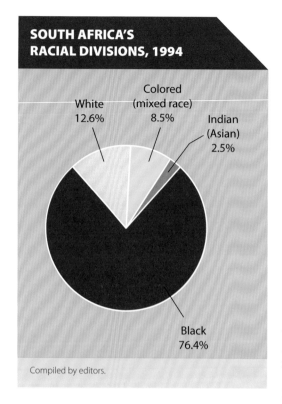

SOUTH AFRICA'S RACIAL DIVISIONS, 1994

White 12.6%

Colored (mixed race) 8.5%

Indian (Asian) 2.5%

Black 76.4%

Compiled by editors.

This chart shows the breakdown of racial classification in South Africa at the time of its first all-races national election in 1994. The total population was estimated at 43.9 million people.

Only after such a referendum, and if the result is positive, will implementation follow. I also wish to emphasise that only Parliament as constituted at present has the power to amend the present Constitution. . . .

There is suspicion that the Government's proposal concerning transitional government is designed to ensure continued domination by Whites or at least to the drawn-out withholding of full participation by Black South Africans.

I wish to put it clearly that there are no grounds for this suspicion. The Government is not playing games with this important issue. Its proposal is motivated on the one hand by the genuine conviction that the final negotiation of a comprehensive and all-embracing constitution will be best achieved under circumstances in which no party will be able to be accused of abusing governmental power to further its own interests. Only the institution of a transitional government that is broadly representative of the entire population will be able to ensure that.

The same applies to Parliament. Preferably the total population should participate in it through their elected representatives in order to create the required confidence. Therefore, when negotiations on a transitional government take place, we propose that Parliament be looked at simultaneously.

What the Government envisages is a transitional government that will be subject to Parliamentary control and which will have to submit legislation to Parliament. That is the essence of democracy. Government by decree is not acceptable. Parliament has to be a fully-fledged part of every phase of constitutional change. . . .

Bill of Fundamental Rights

A new constitution cannot be separated from a bill of fundamental rights. The Government is committed to the principle of a justiciable bill of fundamental rights as part of a new constitutional dispensation. That is why it took the initiative that led to the recent publication of the South African Law Commission's Interim Report on Group and Human Rights.

In conjunction with this, the Government has also taken the initiative of making a study of international conventions on fundamental rights, including the rights of women and children and the United Nations Declaration on Human Rights. We have already progressed a long way with this in the realisation that it is necessary for South Africa to come into line with the international community. . . .

> If everyone were to sweep before his own door and stop undermining the South African Police . . . things will improve very quickly.

Everyone Must Contribute

It is essential for every [South African political] leader to assume joint responsibility for ending the climate of violence.

They have to stop seeking all the blame elsewhere and should take greater pains to motivate their followers to peaceful behaviour.

Mass actions, which so often lead to violence, have to be kept to a minimum. Where they do occur, they have to be better managed and controlled.

Inciting speeches and pronouncements have to cease

and the letter and spirit of the Peace Accord have to be honoured.

If everyone were to sweep before his own door and stop undermining the South African Police and placing it under suspicion, things will improve very quickly.

It is unjustified to try to put the blame for the current violence, particularly in the Black residential areas, on the security forces. On the contrary, all political leaders owe a debt of gratitude and appreciation to our security forces and should go out of their way to boost their confidence and morale.

Only if the masses respect our men and women in uniform and have confidence in them will they be able to be fully effective. Only if political leaders are responsible in their utterances about our security forces will the masses develop that confidence and respect.

Naturally mistakes are made in the security forces. Certainly individual members do not always act faultlessly—neither in other countries nor in South Africa. In such cases there are adequate mechanisms for investigating allegations of improper involvement in violence by members of the security forces. . . .

Sympathy to the Police and to Civilians

I wish to pay tribute to the members of the Police Force who gave their lives for a better South Africa. We honour their memory. We express our sincere sympathy with their next of kin. Their deaths are a great loss to us.

At the same time I wish to express my sincere sympathy on behalf of the Government to all civilian South Africans who lost loved ones in this period of political violence. Their deaths are an indictment of all those who do not wish to honestly take the road of negotiation which is now open to everybody.

May this tragic chapter in our history move everyone to positive action towards ensuring the success of the negotiation process as soon as possible. Therein lies the solution. . . .

> The ending of our isolation has become irreversible.

The World Moves Toward Progress

The opportunities offered by the lifting of sanctions on a global basis, the opening of new markets, the reciprocal attention by other countries to the markets offered by South Africa and the growing number of countries in which there is an official South African presence, heighten the Government's direct concern in the momentous global changes which have marked, and will continue to mark, the last decade of the Twentieth Century.

It is a pity, therefore, that certain elements in South Africa are still persisting with their efforts to delay the normalisation of South Africa's international relations. Those who are doing so, are swimming against the tide. In spite of a temporary success here and there, they are rapidly losing the grip they once had on the foreign policies of many countries towards South Africa. The world outside wishes to see orderly reform succeed and are critical of elements that are negative. The ending of our isolation has become irreversible.

We cannot afford to waste any time in this regard. Together with other African States, we have to adjust to a new situation. A cold war between two superpowers has given way to a completely new situation. We are now living in a world in which the term superpower no longer has a purely military overtone but also implies economic performance and human development. . . .

A Great Test Looms, and the Country Must Pass

Today we are looking back on two significant years of dramatic sea change. As I have indicated, however, it was also a period in which a deliberate foundation was laid

At the final session of South Africa's whites-only House of Assembly on December 22, 1993, President F.W. de Klerk, left, smiles alongside Prisons Minister Adriaan Volk, center, and Minister of Defense and Justice Kobie Coetsee. (**AP Images.**)

for the achievement of our goals of peace, prosperity, progress and participation by all.

All of this has placed us before one of the greatest tests in the history of our country—the test to succeed in honestly negotiating a new constitutional dispensation.

There are some political parties and organisations that are still shying away from it. They ought to know that their refusal to take part will not halt the changes. What has been begun, has to be concluded. Without successful negotiations, long-term peace and prosperity cannot be assured.

> To all South Africans my message is: Bear up!

There are others who are taking part, but who, at the same time, are acting by way of their utterances and mass actions, as if they are not participating. Their actions are in conflict with the spirit of negotiation and are contrary to the agreements already reached. They must know that the Government will not allow itself to be steam-rollered or intimidated. All they are achieving is to undermine the credibility of negotiation. If this continues, it will inevitably delay progress.

The Government is determined to make 1992 a year of significant progress. It can be done.

To all South Africans my message is: Bear up! Through constructive negotiation we shall establish a new dispensation that will offer security and justice to every section of our population. We shall not be satisfied with anything less.

Be strong in keeping faith. Our future is in the Hands of an Almighty and Merciful God.

The United Nations Drops Economic Sanctions

UN Chronicle

The following selection from an official United Nations publication summarizes the effectiveness of international sanctions against South Africa and marks their end. The sanctions began in 1962. They ended after the country moved to become a democracy in 1994. The article also notes that two South Africans—Nelson Mandela and F.W. de Klerk—shared the 1993 Nobel Peace Prize.

Noting that the "transition to democracy has now been enshrined in the law of South Africa", the General Assembly [of the United Nations] on 8 October ended a 31-year ban on economic and other

---

SOURCE. *UN Chronicle* Contributors, "Sanctions Lifted After 31 Years," *UN Chronicle*, vol. 31, March 1994, pp. 49–50. Copyright © 1994 United Nations. Reprinted with the permission of the United Nations.

Nelson Mandela, left, and F.W. de Klerk shared the 1993 Nobel Peace Prize. (**AP Images.**)

ties with South Africa and its nationals, in the areas of trade, investment, finance, travel and transportation. States were asked to lift the sanctions they had imposed over the years under numerous UN resolutions and decisions.

Economic sanctions were first enacted in 1962, when the Assembly asked Member States to break off diplomatic relations with South Africa, boycott its goods and refrain from exporting goods, including armaments, to that country. Those sanctions were expanded over the years, as the international community sought to end the system of apartheid, which the Assembly had repeatedly condemned as a "crime against humanity".

In adopting resolution 48/1 by consensus, the 184-member world body decided that the embargo on petroleum and petroleum products and on investment in the petroleum industry in South Africa would cease,

> 'The long journey towards the final obliteration of over 300 years of minority domination is near its end.'

as soon as the Transitional Executive Council—South Africa's first non-racial governing body—became operational. That Council met for the first time on 7 December in Cape Town.

Ibrahim A. Gambari of Nigeria, Chairman of the Special Committee against Apartheid, said the Assembly action would send "a very strong signal" to South Africans that the international community would assist in the country's economic reconstruction and ensure that the new South Africa would begin its existence unhampered by the constraints imposed on the old South Africa. "The long journey towards the final obliteration of over 300 years of minority domination is near its end", he later said.

Years of UN Pressure Achieve Results

The Security Council instituted a voluntary arms embargo against South Africa in 1963, making it mandatory on 4 November 1977—the first time such an action had been taken against a Member State.

Also in 1977, the Assembly asked the Council to consider imposing mandatory economic sanctions and in January 1979, to consider a mandatory embargo on oil and oil products.

The International Convention against Apartheid in Sports, adopted by the Assembly in 1985, entered into force on 4 April 1988. The Convention obliged States parties not to permit sports contacts with countries practising apartheid.

In November 1986, the Assembly set up the Intergovernmental Group to Monitor the Supply and Shipping of Oil and Petroleum Products to South Africa. Its mandate was terminated on 20 December 1993.

In December 1991, following positive steps taken by South Africa, including repeal and revision of major apartheid and security laws, the Assembly declared that academic, scientific and cultural links could be resumed with South Africa, provided they were with democratic, anti-apartheid organizations. It also declared sports contacts with non-racial South African sporting organizations could resume.

On 9 October [1993], the Security Council increased the number of UN observers by 40, to 100, to reinforce security and stability in the country during the transitional period. By the April [1994] elections, close to 2,000 observers of the UN Observer Mission in South Africa (UNOMSA) are expected to be in South Africa.

> [UN Secretary-General Boutros Boutros-Ghali] congratulated all South Africans who supported the peace process despite 'many impediments' amid mounting violence and intimidation.

The Final Steps Occur

On 20 December [1993], the Assembly adopted four additional resolutions *(48/159 A to 48/159 D)* on the elimination of apartheid and establishment of a united, democratic and non-racial South Africa, and another resolution *(48/160)* on the UN Educational Training Programme for Southern Africa.

Among other things, the Assembly called upon all signatories to the National Peace Accord to recommit themselves to democratic principles, take part in the elections, and resolve outstanding issues by peaceful means only; strongly urged South African authorities to end the ongoing violence; demanded the immediate release of remaining political prisoners; and appealed for increased international humanitarian and legal assistance to apartheid victims.

The Security Council on 23 November welcomed the successful completion on 17 November of the multiparty negotiating process in South Africa, and agreements reached therein on an interim constitution and electoral bill which, it said, constituted a "historic step forward" in establishing a democratic, non-racial and united South Africa.

A Crowning Achievement Is Noted

On 18 November [1993], the Secretary-General [Boutros Boutros-Ghali] applauded the agreement on an interim constitution for the country's transition to democracy which, he said, "crowns three years of very difficult negotiations". He congratulated all South Africans who supported the peace process despite "many impediments" amid mounting violence and intimidation. The UN was ready to assist in the "formidable challenges that lay ahead", including the country's first multiparty democratic elections.

The interim constitution will serve as South Africa's supreme law, until a permanent constitution is adopted by a constituent assembly to be elected in its first "one-person-one-vote" elections in April. That document—a culmination of years of negotiations—is to guarantee fundamental rights, including the right to vote, for all South Africans, regardless of race.

In a statement *(S/26785)* by Council President José Luis Jesus of Cape Verde, the 15-member body urged all parties in South Africa, including those which did not participate fully in the multiparty talks, to respect agreements reached during the negotiations, recommit themselves to democratic principles, take part in the elections, and resolve outstanding issues by peaceful means only.

The Council considered that South Africa's transition to democracy must be underpinned by economic and social reconstruction and development, and called on the international community to assist in that regard.

> The [UN] Special Committee [against apartheid] shared the hopes of all South Africans for a peaceful transition to a non-racial and democratic society.

On 16 December, Lakhdar Brahimi, former Algerian Foreign Minister, was named the Secretary-General's Special Representative for South Africa.

The Special Committee against Apartheid, also on 18 November, expressed the hope that parties which had suspended participation in negotiations would continue to participate in a peaceful dialogue within the multiparty process and take part in the electoral process. It asked parties to refrain from acts that would jeopardize South Africa's first non-racial election.

The Special Committee shared the hopes of all South Africans for a peaceful transition to a non-racial and democratic society.

The Secretary-General, in Maputo, Mozambique in mid-October, conducted a series of meetings with, among others, South African Foreign Minister Pik Botha, Chief Mangosuthu Buthelezi, President of the Inkatha Freedom Party and Chief Minister of Kwazulu, Clarence Makwetu, President of the Pan Africanist Congress of Azania (PAC), John Hall, Chairperson of the National Peace Committee, and Anthony Gildenhuys, Chairperson of the National Peace Secretariat.

Joint Peace Prize Winners Are Declared

On 15 October, it was announced that the 1993 Nobel Peace Prize would be awarded to South African President F.W. de Klerk and ANC [African National Congress] President Nelson Mandela. The Prize was presented on 10 December at a ceremony in Oslo, Norway.

The Secretary-General applauded "those two courageous leaders" who were working together, along with the people of South Africa, to eradicate the evil of apartheid.

General Assembly President [Samuel] Insanally said the two statesmen had the "vision and determination to move towards a democratic and non-racial government in South Africa through the process of dialogue and negotiations".

Special Committee Chairman Gambari said the award was "an encouragement to those who have the moral strength, steadfastness and generosity to overcome the deep wounds of oppression inflicted by apartheid in order to seek reconciliation and to build a new future of justice, dignity and prosperity for all South Africans".

The 1993 recipients join two other South African Nobel Peace laureates—former ANC President Albert Luthuli and Archbishop Desmond Tutu.

The Truth and Reconciliation Commission Is Established

The Parliament of South Africa

This selection is an excerpt of one of the most extraordinary government acts in world history. After decades of official oppression of nonwhite people, South Africa declared it would create a Truth and Reconciliation Commission. Through this commission, the government would publicize its own injustices, including killings by government agents, and would grant amnesty to those who fully disclosed their participation. It would also recognize individual victims and try to grant reparations.

SOURCE. The Parliament of South Africa, "Promotion of National Unity and Reconciliation Act of 1995," South African Government (www.doj.gov.za), July 26, 1995. © GCIS2004. All rights reserved. Reproduced by permission.

At the first hearing before the Truth and Reconciliation Commission, Nohle Mohapi is sworn in as the commission's first witness. She testified about the death in detention of her husband, Mapetla Mohapi. (**AP Images.**)

To provide for the investigation and the establishment of as complete a picture as possible of the nature, causes and extent of gross violations of human rights committed during the period from 1 March 1960 to the cut-off date contemplated in the Constitution, within or outside the Republic, emanating from the conflicts of the past, and the fate or whereabouts of the victims of such violations; the granting of amnesty to persons who make full disclosure of all the relevant facts relating to acts associated with a political objective committed in the course of the conflicts of the past during the said period; affording victims an opportunity to relate the violations they suffered; the taking of measures aimed at the granting of reparation to, and the rehabilitation and the restoration of the human and civil dignity of, victims of violations of human rights; reporting to the Nation about such violations and victims; the making of recommendations aimed at the prevention of the commission of gross violations of human rights; and for the said purposes to provide for the establishment of a Truth and Reconciliation Commission, a Committee on Human Rights Violations, a Committee on Amnesty and a Committee on Reparation and Rehabilitation; and to confer certain powers on, assign certain functions to and impose certain duties upon that Commission and those Committees; and to provide for matters connected therewith.

> "There is a need for understanding but not for vengeance, a need for reparation but not for retaliation."

SINCE the Constitution of the Republic of South Africa, 1993 (Act No. 200 of 1993), provides a historic bridge between the past of a deeply divided society characterized by strife, conflict, untold suffering and injustice, and a future founded on the recognition of human rights, democracy and peaceful co-existence for all South Africans, irrespective of colour, race, class, belief or sex;

AND SINCE it is deemed necessary to establish the truth in relation to past events as well as the motives for and circumstances in which gross violations of human fights have occurred, and to make the findings known in order to prevent a repetition of such acts in future;

AND SINCE the Constitution states that the pursuit of national unity, the well-being of all South African citizens and peace require reconciliation between the people of South Africa and the reconstruction of society;

AND SINCE the Constitution states that there is a need for understanding but not for vengeance, a need for reparation but not for retaliation, a need for ubuntu [African concept of human generosity] but not for victimization;

AND SINCE the Constitution states that in order to advance such reconciliation and reconstruction amnesty shall be granted in respect of acts, omissions and offences associated with political objectives committed in the course of the conflicts of the past;

AND SINCE the Constitution provides that Parliament shall under the Constitution adopt a law which determines a firm cut-off date, which shall be a date after 8 October 1990 and before the cut-off date envisaged in the Constitution, and providing for the mechanisms, criteria and procedures, including tribunals, if any, through which such amnesty shall be dealt with;

BE IT THEREFORE ENACTED by the Parliament of the Republic of South Africa.

CHAPTER 2

Controversies Surrounding the End of Apartheid

The Case Is Made for Worldwide Opposition to Apartheid

Albert J. Lutuli and Martin Luther King, Jr.

In this joint statement, Albert J. Lutuli and Martin Luther King, Jr., civil rights pioneers from South Africa and the United States, appeal for international action against apartheid. Both men believed in nonviolent resistance, a method employed earlier in South Africa by Mahatma Gandhi before he led a struggle for independence in India.

Zulu Chief Albert J. Lutuli became president of the African National Congress in 1952 and won the 1960 Nobel Peace Prize. The Rev. Dr. Martin Luther King, Jr. became president of the Southern Christian Leadership Conference in 1957 and won the 1964 Nobel Peace Prize.

Photo on previous page: In Cape Town, a painting depicting Hendrik Verwoerd (standing second from right, known as the architect of apartheid and later prime minister) and his cabinet, is removed from the South African parliament building's old assembly wing lobby. (**AP Images.**)

SOURCE. Albert J. Lutuli and Martin Luther King, Jr., "Appeal for Action Against Apartheid," *African National Congress*, 1962. Reproduced by permission.

In 1957, an unprecedented Declaration of Conscience was issued by more than 100 leaders from every continent. That Declaration was an appeal to South Africa to bring its policies into line with the Universal Declaration of Human Rights adopted by the General Assembly of the United Nations.

The Declaration was a good start in mobilizing world sentiment to back those in South Africa who acted for equality. The non-whites took heart in learning that they were not alone. And many white supremacists learned for the first time how isolated they were.

Subsequent to the Declaration, the South African Government took the following measures:

Albert John Luthuli, former Zulu chief, was a civil rights pioneer from South Africa and won the Nobel Peace Prize in 1960. (Keystone/Getty Images.)

- BANNED the African National Congress and the Pan Africanist Congress, the principal protest organisations, and jailed their leaders;

- COERCED the press into strict pro-government censorship and made it almost impossible for new anti-apartheid publications to exist;

- ESTABLISHED an arms industry, more than tripled the military budget, distributed small arms to the white population, enlarged the army, created an extensive white civilian militia;

- ACTIVATED total physical race separation by establishing the first Bantustan in the Transkei with the aid of emergency police regulations;

- LEGALLY DEFINED protest against apartheid as an act of "sabotage," an offense ultimately punishable by death;

- PERPETUATED its control through terrorism and violence:

  - Human Rights Day (December 10), 1959—12 South West Africans killed at Windhock and 40 wounded as they fled police

  - March 21, 1960—72 Africans killed and 186 wounded at Sharpeville by police

  - Before and during the two-year "emergency" in the Transkei—15 Africans killed by police, thousands arrested and imprisoned without trial.

Peaceful Action Is Needed

The deepening tensions can lead to two alternatives:

Solution: Intensified persecution may lead to violence and armed rebellion once it is clear that peaceful adjustments are no longer possible. As the persecution has been inflicted by one racial group upon all other racial groups, large-scale violence would take the form of a racial war.

This "solution" may be workable. But mass racial extermination will destroy the potential for interracial unity in South Africa and elsewhere.

Therefore, we ask for your action to make the following possible.

Solution 2: "Nothing which we have suffered at the hands of the government has turned us from our chosen path of disciplined resistance," said Chief Albert J. Lutuli at Oslo. So there exists another alternative—and the only solution which represents sanity—transition to a society based upon equality for all without regard to colour.

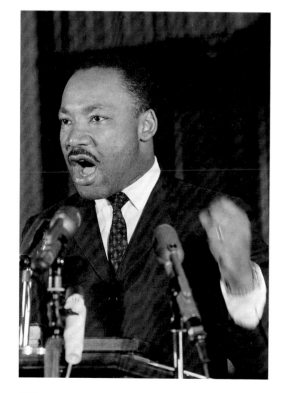

The Rev. Martin Luther King, Jr., delivers an address in Selma, Alabama, on February 22, 1965. (AP Images.)

Any solution founded on justice is unattainable until the Government of South Africa is forced by pressures, both internal and external, to come to terms with the demands of the non-white majority.

> We . . . ask all men of goodwill to take action against apartheid.

The apartheid republic is a reality today *only because* the peoples and governments of the world have been unwilling to place her in quarantine.

Soweto, a Home of Opposition

The struggle against apartheid found fertile ground in the hardscrabble Johannesburg suburb called Soweto. The name is derived from the area's official designation, South Western Townships.

At first a temporary living area for mine workers, Soweto grew as an enforced black ghetto full of shack dwellers. Eventually an estimated three million people lived in Soweto, which is less than 25 square miles. Some schools, hospitals, and more substantial homes were built. But poverty, crime, and repression marked much of Soweto's history.

Nelson Mandela and his wife Winnie lived there in the 1950s and early 1960s, before he was imprisoned. For a time, Desmond Tutu lived on the same street.

Soweto contains Avalon Cemetery, where thousands of metal cots mark graves. This stems from an old custom of burial in hard-stone areas, where graves could not be dug deeply and so rocks were placed over the corpses to protect them from animals. Also in Soweto is Freedom Square, as it is now called, where the Freedom Charter was adopted as the guiding document of the African National Congress.

Translate Public Opinion into Public Action

We, therefore, ask all men of goodwill to take action against apartheid in the following manner:

Hold meetings and demonstrations on December 10, Human Rights Day;

Urge your church, union, lodge, or club to observe this day as one of protest;

Urge your Government to support economic sanctions;

Write to your mission to the United Nations urging adoption of a resolution calling for international isolation of South Africa;

Don't buy South Africa's products;

Don't trade or invest in South Africa;

Translate public opinion into public action by explaining facts to all peoples, to groups to which you belong, and to countries of which you are citizens until an effective international quarantine of apartheid is established.

The Prime Minister Describes Apartheid's Benefits

Hendrik F. Verwoerd

In this excerpt from a major 1963 speech, South Africa's prime minister, Hendrik F. Verwoerd, vigorously defends white rule as the foundation for generations of greatness. He denies there is government oppression in South Africa and says other nations are hypocrites for condemning apartheid. Verwoerd cites the difficulties experienced in African nations that gained independence from white rule, and he alleges that attempts to create multiracial societies in the United States and United Kingdom failed.

Verwoerd, known as the architect of apartheid, became South Africa's cabinet member in charge of native affairs in 1950 and was prime minister from 1958 to 1966.

SOURCE. Hendrik F. Verwoerd, "Crisis in World Conscience," *Crisis in World Conscience and the Road to Freedom for Basutoland, Bechuanaland, Swaziland*, 1963, pp. 1–6, 8–10. Copyright © 2004 GCIS. All rights reserved. Reproduced by permission.

Hendrik Verwoerd, was known as the architect of apartheid and later prime minister of South Africa from 1958 to 1966. (**Popperfoto/Getty Images**.)

During the past five years [1958–63] we have seen the continuation of tremendous economic progress and further expansion of practically every industry of importance to the country. We have seen the rise of the chemical industry. Lately we have witnessed the establishment of a vast new copper-mining venture to which further expansion of our fertilizer and chemical industries, perhaps even our steel industry is linked.

We have witnessed impressive new plans for the generation of electricity and the expansion of the steel industry. There has been progress in every field of industry that is basic to the needs of the nation. More and more gold is being mined for the world-market, where there is an acute need for it. In every field of manufacture, even in the production of food, we are making progress.

> For each nation the golden age came at a time when great demands were being made upon it.

Difficulties experienced in connection with our balance of payments and monetary reserves were tackled and solved during these five years. Tackled to such good effect, indeed, that South Africa is today regarded, in relation to its size, as one of the most prosperous and richest countries of the world.

In a way these five years can be seen as the beginning of our golden age.

When one takes a look at world history, one realizes that the golden ages of nations were never the easiest. For each nation the golden age came at a time when great demands were being made upon it, when it was compelled to work hard and to make sacrifices of all kinds. During the past five years we likewise experienced difficulties, but have now reached the stage where we are riding on the crest of a growing wave of prosperity.

The Unity of Whites Is Strong

But it is not only in the economic field that we have achieved our objectives. In the constitutional sphere we have reached fulfilment of ideals and have come to a better understanding of their intrinsic worth. South Africa has become a Republic. We have left the [British] Commonwealth. And this Republic outside the Commonwealth has become to us not so much the attainment of an ideal as the foundation upon which we aspire to build a great country for a great nation of the future.

As a result we are also in the process of achieving what many thought impossible: the growth of a single nation with greater, stronger and more lasting bonds of unity between the White groups in South Africa.

A spiritual change is taking place; it is gripping us and inspiring us. Those from outside our borders who think they need only exert pressure to bring this government to a downfall because they believe it does not enjoy the support of almost half of the nation—they are thinking of the English-speaking half—are now beginning to realise that supporting this ideal of national unity, and aiming at the continued existence of a White nation in South Africa, there will be found almost the entire White population of the country. This impressive unity is of paramount importance to our nation—of far greater importance than we ourselves sometimes realise.

The Military and Police Are Powerful

During this period we have seen not only economic development, constitutional change, spiritual change, and growth towards unity, but also the increase of our country's strength. Just consider the means at our disposal should South Africa have to protect herself against attacks from outside, or should she be obliged to act against attempts to undermine law and order within her borders. Hardly ever before has there been such an expansion of our defence forces and such an improvement in their equipment. Hardly ever before has there been such an advance in the size and efficiency of our police force. We can be justifiably proud—as, indeed, we are—of the way in which the forces of law and order, guardians of the safety of the state against those that are envious of it, have developed during this period.

> We wish to separate the races so that each individual can enjoy all rights and opportunities among his own people.

A start has also been made with projects in our country which are both vast and of far-reaching significance. . . . The face of the whole of the southern part of South Africa will be changed as a result of a blueprint of development on a scale that has never before been undertaken here. It is a forty-year plan—which proves our determination to keep the control of White South Africa in our hands for this generation and for future generations.

The first five years have passed like a dream, because they were momentous years full of action and hard work. And we believe that these years were but the beginning of a future upon which we can enter with equanimity, knowing that it is based on firm foundations.

Our Race Relations Problem Is Complex

Our major task is to ensure that a White nation will prevail here. Every nation has the inalienable right to safeguard that which it has built for itself and for posterity. This, then, is our task. But it is clear that we have also to deal with an immense problem closely related to this— that of race relations. No other nation would appear to have a race relations problem as complicated and of such magnitude as the one with which we have to cope.

It is our aim to survive and to prosper as a White nation, but we know that this cannot be done by suppressing those entrusted to our care; neither can they be denied the opportunity to develop fully. This is a lesson that history has taught us, and which we know only too well. It is disgraceful, therefore, that the outside world associates the concept of separate development with oppression.

> When we look at the world around us, we find practically all nations condemning our policy.

If the word *apartheid* was chosen with any aim at all at the time by Dr. D.F. Malan then it was done to say, both to the Whites and the Blacks and indeed to the whole world, that we do *not* seek to oppress; we do not seek separation in our interests alone. We wish to separate the races so that each individual can enjoy all rights and opportunities among his own people, and where possible, in his own territory. Its objective is friendly, born out of goodwill. Yet the outside world, and even those we call our friends, are not prepared to accept this clear definition of "apartheid". They go out of their way—every time they use abusive language against us—to say dogmatically: apartheid is oppression, born out of race hatred.

Our Enemies Are Everywhere

It is important for us to take note of what is being done against South Africa in the outside world. Little that is new can be said on this subject. I would, however, like to turn the spotlight on a few facts in connection with the world attitude towards South Africa. Since it is our task—one of the utmost importance—to maintain our position, it becomes necessary to investigate the influences which seek to thwart our objectives and even to destroy our work.

When we look at the world around us, we find practically all nations condemning our policy. We find that organisations such as the United Nations condemn us—often in drastic terms. On the other hand, when trade is under consideration, there is a greater appreciation of South Africa's value among countries that are sometimes our severest critics, as well as in the world in general. They do realise that South Africa is *not* a danger to world peace; they realise also that South Africa provides, and aims at providing, increasingly better services for its non-Whites, services unequalled by any other nation. In commercial relationships these countries act on the basis of this knowledge rather than in accordance with the verbal attacks on us. They expect South Africans to be "mature and sensible enough" not to feel too hurt and not to be goaded into "irresponsible action" by the language hurled at us under the cloak of friendship.

South Africans happen to be a level-headed nation. They do not allow themselves to be driven into emotional reactions or tension by what is said against them. They take into account the realities of life, and are conscious of the justice of their cause and of their value to others. That is why they do not allow themselves to be driven to irresponsible language and action in return. Yet nobody, not even the great powers, should believe that we fail to observe the double standards applied by them when they deal with matters affecting our country. Neither must they think that the measure of our respect for them is not influenced by what we observe. We are clear-headed and tolerant, but we also make our own deductions and see what is happening.

> "Afro-Asian nations, in an effort to divert the attention from their own shortcomings, attack prosperous South Africa."

We Stand Against Communism and for Christianity

We ask ourselves why we are condemned by others. As far as the Communist countries are concerned, we can understand the reasons only too well. Since Russia and other countries associated with her want the communist ideology to triumph in the world, they must create unrest and chaos wherever possible. Therefore it is necessary for them to eliminate any forces of resistance to their attempts and to destroy those countries that serve as anchors against the drift towards their ideology.

South Africa is unequivocally the symbol of anti-Communism in Africa. Although often abused, we are also still a bastion in Africa for Christianity and the Western world.

It is therefore understandable that the Communists should employ their usual methods against South Africa:

to create suspicion, to brand the country as a threat to world peace, to say that we are aggressive and to describe our government or policy as oppressive. Such is the pattern of their attacks on other countries of the West: Germany, Britain, and the United States of America. Consequently, it is not surprising to find them encouraging those countries of Africa that come under their influence—albeit ideologically and not yet openly acknowledged—to launch the same kind of attack on us. We realise that they are attacking South Africa as a stronghold of the West in Africa and that these attacks by the Communists, in their attempts to subject the world to their ideology, will continue.

> The issue at stake is the self-preservation of a nation.

We Are a Scapegoat

The second group of attackers is the African and Asian states. Many of their leaders are still novices in politics and administration. They have yet to prove to their own people the value of their newly acquired freedom. They must prove that they can now become prosperous and that on their own they can earn a better living, build better houses and schools and have better health services and produce a greater variety of consumer goods. Because they have not succeeded in proving their ability and progress in these spheres, they must prevent their own people from suspecting that they are not able to do better than, or even as well as, their predecessors, the Whites, who governed before them.

They must find a scapegoat somewhere, somehow. They must keep emotions and expectations alive. After all, the new rulers themselves came to power as a result of incitement and the raising of false hopes. From this it becomes clear why these Afro-Asian nations, in an effort to divert the attention from their own shortcomings, attack prosperous South Africa, more especially since the opportunity is provided by the vacillating attitude of Western nations, which we still find hard to understand.

Why the West Opposes Us

But why do the Western nations, from whom we are descended and with whom we have such close cultural ties, turn against us?

The reason is not to be found in any deep inner conviction that we are wrong, or that we are oppressors, despite the fact that they use these accusations against us. They have other reasons. They know that no matter how much sympathy they may have for South Africa, or how unreasonable they may regard the treatment meted out to us, they have to consider certain interests of their own. These interests are closely related to the fact that the numerical strength of the Afro-Asians, combined with that of the Communist states, makes their influence such that they can dominate decisions on world politics. The number of votes to be gained at the United Nations is never let out of sight. . . .

The Western nations also consider the economic advantages that can result from closer links with these states as producers of raw materials or as potential customers. It is for political and economic reasons, and also to further their own interests, that the Western nations follow this line of action on South Africa.

Why We Must Stay the Course

I know that there are critics in the Republic who want us to take note of this unfavourable sentiment towards us, and to bow to so-called world opinion because, they say, South Africa cannot stand alone. Being aware, however, of the nature of the opposition abroad to our policies, and why such world opinion as there is has been instigated against us, we must ask the question: how can we conciliate this attitude of Governments and at what price?

The reply is that such world opinion or governmental attitudes—in reality based on Communist designs, on the Afro-Asian aspirations to share in the riches of Southern Africa for which they want the one-man-one-vote principle, and on the selfish interests of the Western nations—would have us hand over the land of our fathers to black domination.

It then becomes immediately obvious that critics who say that we must bow to such pressure are expecting the impossible.

The issue at stake is the self-preservation of a nation—nothing more and nothing less. It is also the self-preservation of each individual member of this White nation. This we in South Africa understand fully. We are therefore on our guard against making more and more concessions which could eventually lead to the loss of everything we cherish, and which will ultimately prove to be of importance to others: the West and also our non-White wards.

When we put our case so specifically, we are told that we are too narrow-minded, that we do not heed a world conscience which is inspired by ideals of peace and freedom.

What Happens When Blacks Take Over

When one looks at what is happening in the world, the question arises, however, whether there is in fact a world conscience that is really concerned over the ideals of peace and freedom. Let us subject the "world conscience" as manifested in the United Nations to the acid test of reality.

The first test is to take a closer look at the nations that have gained their independence and at the manner in which they uphold freedom. At the same time the extent to which the world and the United Nations ensure

> It becomes 'Freedom' when any black group rules, come what may! Even black tyranny is Freedom!

that real freedom is maintained there must be considered. What happens in those states of Africa that have become free? For conscience sake they had to be liberated from White governments even where these governments had brought the people prosperity. When Black governments took over, individual freedom should

> History has shown that where there are vast differences between people, there can be no peace and co-operation on the road to integration.

have been maintained or, rather, increased. Did anybody, or any state, really object when a Black government fell into the hands of a small group or of a single dictator? Was the United Nations vehemently urged to act when opposition members were arrested and opposition parties destroyed? Or do we find that such issues are whitewashed by calling such a state not a dictatorship but "a one-party state in keeping with the character of Africa"?

Freedom, mutilated as in Ghana, chaotic as in the Congo, or illusory as we can see it in Liberia and Ethiopia—where the masses, in addition, live in misery—is not true freedom.

The morality of "world opinion", of a world organisation or of the great powers is exposed in all its cynical nakedness when these conditions are tolerated or ignored. It becomes "Freedom" when any black group rules, come what may! Even black tyranny is Freedom!

In this first test the world, which adopts a high moral pose when dealing with South Africa, fails miserably to prove that it has a conscience or a single standard and that it acts accordingly. . . .

The U.S. Compares Unfavorably to South Africa

The Whites in South Africa can see clearly what is expected of them. Whatever the cost, they must continue to survive until such time as the West experiences a change of heart.

Let us compare this course with what is happening in countries with which we are closely linked. I want to name only two: the United States of America and the United Kingdom. If we examine the accusation that our approach is wrong and that we should take our cue from them, do we find in their example a solution for the problem of race relations?

The United States does not tolerate legislation aimed at separation, separate development, differentiation, apartheid, or whatever you wish to call it, although much still remains with them as a heritage from their own past. Americans say they do not advocate segregation; they want to legislate against separation. In other words they want to enforce multi-racialism by means of legislation.

What results can they show for the process of desegregation which began many years ago? Has this brought a solution to the problem where only about ten per cent of their population is non-White? Have their methods of integration brought peace and an end to discrimination? Have these means bred friendship, love and co-operation? If we are to travel the road of multi-racialism, can we find any encouragement from the results achieved in the United States, where the proportion of non-Whites in relation to Whites is so much smaller than in South Africa?

> By separating we aim at the same high objectives that others seek through integration.

Here in the Republic we have greater peace and order. We have much less rude handling, or oppression, and far less ill-feeling between Black and White. History has shown that where there are vast differences between people, there can be no peace and co-operation on the road to integration. People, however different, can on the other hand co-operate when they live in separate states and are able to deal with one another on that basis. This is also possible when, in the same state, each person seeks his destiny among his own people. Then there can be peace, co-operation and—for each group—its own purpose in life. This one does not find in a mixed community forced to act as if it were united.

The British Also Fail

The experience of Great Britain proves the same point. Where in Britain did they succeed in avoiding trouble when significant numbers of non-Whites settled in a community? The influx of even a small number of non-Whites has prompted local authorities to warn against "the rise of racial hatred in Britain". Riots have occurred in various places in England. This proves again that multi-racialism simply does not provide a solution.

Let us consider British policy in Africa. Here the policy was partnership—"you must co-operate, you must learn to understand and appreciate one another; you need not necessarily inter-marry; but you must live in harmony with one another, because politically you are partners".

What has become of partnership in Kenya and Tanganyika [now Tanzania]? In Nyasaland [Malawi] and Northern Rhodesia [Zambia]? Where are the White partners? How much trouble is this policy not causing in Southern Rhodesia [Zimbabwe]? Surely Britain cannot contend that her policy of multi-racialism has led to a successful solution for all former inhabitants of those countries. Indeed, this experiment teaches us what we should not do.

When, therefore, I view the situation as it exists in other countries—countries with whom we wish to retain cordial relations—I can only say that their experiences have taught us to seek a different approach.

We do not take the road of oppression, and we also wish to remove discrimination. Our policy provides for a proper and independent existence for the Whites. At the same time it seeks to accord the same privileges—in different ways—to all the non-Whites now living in our country. By separating we aim at the same high objectives that others seek through integration. The objectives are similar; the methods differ fundamentally. For this country we have no doubt that our methods alone can ultimately prove fair to all races, including the Whites. Other countries must choose for themselves.

South Africans Support Sanctions to Bring an End to Apartheid

Desmond Tutu

The following selection is adapted from a commencement address at Hunter College in New York City, given by South African apartheid foe Desmond Tutu, the 1984 Nobel Peace Prize winner. He asserts that sanctions are needed to force the South African government to change. He describes as "baloney" the arguments made by some international companies that their presence in South Africa has actually improved the lives of black South Africans. Tutu insists that while sanctions may make life difficult in South Africa, the devastation resulting from a civil war—the likely outcome if the government does not dismantle apartheid—would be far worse. Desmond Tutu's achievements include becoming an Anglican archbishop and heading South Africa's Truth and Reconciliation Commission.

SOURCE. Desmond Tutu, "Sanctions vs. Apartheid," *The New York Times*, June 16, 1986, p. 19. Copyright © 1986 by The New York Times Company. Reproduced by permission.

A clear message resounds in recent surveys in South Africa in which more than 70 percent of blacks supported sanctions against the Government. Blacks are saying: "We are suffering already. To end it, we will support sanctions, even if we have to take on additional suffering."

Our people have shown they mean business by their use of consumer boycotts. Last year [1985], organizations representing more than 12 million South Africans called for sanctions and economic pressure. These are not insignificant actions or irresponsible bodies or individuals.

I must ask, To whom is the international community willing to listen? To the victims and their spokesmen or to the perpetrators of apartheid and those who benefit from it?

I would be more impressed with those who made no bones about the reason they remain in South Africa and said, honestly, "We are concerned for our profits," instead of the baloney that the businesses are there for our benefit. We don't want you there. Please do us a favor: get out and come back when we have a democratic and just South Africa.

> We do not want apartheid ameliorated or improved. We do not want apartheid made comfortable. We want it dismantled.

Why Some Things Have Improved

It is true that many foreign corporations in South Africa have introduced improvements for their black staff. They now have a better chance of promotion. They get better salaries. But these improvements have come about largely through the pressures of the disinvestment campaign [in which governments and businesses withdrew investments in South Africa]. American companies, especially, have begun to speak out more forthrightly against apartheid than has been their wont, and they would be

the first to admit that they got a considerable jog to their consciences from the disinvestment campaign.

There has been progress, but we do not want apartheid ameliorated or improved. We do not want apartheid made comfortable. We want it dismantled.

You hear people say sanctions don't work. That may be so. But if they don't work, why oppose them so vehemently? If they don't work, why did [British Prime Minister] Margaret Thatcher apply them to Argentina during the Falkland war? Why did the United States apply them to Poland and to Nicaragua? Why was

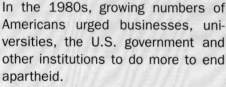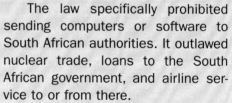

Sanctions and the United States

In the 1980s, growing numbers of Americans urged businesses, universities, the U.S. government and other institutions to do more to end apartheid.

They asked—and sometimes demanded—that these entities stop any economic involvement, including stock ownership, that could benefit South Africa's white leadership.

They also urged the U.S. government to add more pressure to the South African government. President Ronald Reagan's administration favored a low-key approach, but in 1986 Congress passed—over Reagan's veto—a ban on (1) the import of numerous South African products, and (2) American business investment there.

The law specifically prohibited sending computers or software to South African authorities. It outlawed nuclear trade, loans to the South African government, and airline service to or from there.

It declared no American "may, directly or through another person, make any new investment in South Africa."

The sanctions could be lifted if South Africa freed political prisoners, allowed political and personal freedom, negotiated in good faith with black representatives, and moved to dismantle apartheid. The law also called on black groups such as the African National Congress to prevent violence.

President Reagan so annoyed that his European allies did not want to impose sanctions against Libya? If sanctions are so ineffective, why does the United States still maintain a blockade of Cuba? Yet we have all this wonderful sophistry when it comes to South Africa.

I am unaware of anything that has changed in South Africa without pressure. Changes in the sports policy were due to pressure from the sports boycott and not because there had been a change of heart on the part of white sports administrators.

There Is Only One Peaceful Option

We hear some say that sanctions will destroy the South Africa economy and leave us with a financial morass. My response is that the ball is surely in the South African Government's court. Its decisions about the future of the country will determine whether sanctions should be invoked or not. I certainly do not want to destroy a land I love passionately. But if the South African Government remains intransigent and obstinate, then sanctions or no sanctions the economy will be destroyed in the wake of the violence, bloodshed and chaos that will ensue if a full-scale civil war breaks out.

There is no guarantee that sanctions will topple apartheid, but it is the last nonviolent option left, and it is a risk with a chance. President Reagan's policy of constructive engagement, and similar efforts to persuade white South Africans who support apartheid to change, have failed dismally. Let's try another strategy.

There are those who are not ashamed to argue that if they pull out others will come in to exploit black South Africa. The moral turpitude of that argument is quite breathtaking. We are not asking people to make economic or political decisions. We are asking for a moral decision.

There is no room for neutrality. When you say you are neutral in a situation of injustice and oppression, you have decided to support the unjust status quo. Are you on the side of injustice? Are you on the side of oppression or liberation? Are you on the side of death or of life? Are you on the side of goodness or of evil?

Sanctions Wounded Us and Did Not End Apartheid

Helen Suzman

In this excerpt from her memoir, Helen Suzman—long the most prominent white opponent of apartheid—makes the case that sanctions against South Africa were not the right method. Economic growth could have been the engine of change in the country, she says, giving black workers more power. But sanctions caused economic shrinkage and thus job losses, leaving black people worse off.

Suzman was a member of the South African Parliament from 1953 until 1989. For much of that time she was the sole representative of the Progressive Party and the target of Afrikaner intimidation.

SOURCE. Helen Suzman, *No Uncertain Terms: A South African Memoir*. New York: Alfred A. Knopf, 1993. Copyright © 1993 by Helen Suzman. Used by permission of Alfred A. Knopf, Inc., a division of Random House, Inc.

M y opposition to sanctions against South Africa clouded my relationship with many people overseas and with many blacks at home, disappointing those who expected me to be an enthusiastic supporter of punitive action against the regime I opposed over so many years. I believe I had sound economic reasons for my attitude, while as far as the cultural boycott was concerned, it was my belief that contact with the outside world was likely to be more effective than isolation in influencing public opinion in South Africa. . . .

Speaking on campuses or to the Council on Foreign Relations or any other organization in the United States, and in writing articles against sanctions for influential publications such as *The New York Times Magazine*, I emphasized that I understood the sincerity of the moral outrage against apartheid and discriminatory practices in South Africa. After all, had I not been fighting them since my first entrance into Parliament back in 1953? But I did not believe that punitive measures which would wreck the economy and reduce the country to chaos would improve the situation. I understood the desire for punitive action; how often had I sat in Parliament and prayed for divine retribution, but, alas, it soon became obvious that if one lived in South Africa, divine retribution was not selective and that the very people one was hoping to help would be adversely affected by the punitive measures. For that reason the implementation of sanctions, which could only cause the economy to shrink and unemployment to increase, was not the answer. The escalating population explosion, about 3 percent a year in the case of black people, meant that jobs had to be provided for about four hundred thousand young black people each year. If these jobs were not provided, South Africa would face an

> If these jobs [for young black people] were not provided, South Africa would face an era of increased poverty, violence and crime.

Photo on previous page: Helen Suzman, a founding member of South Africa's Progressive Party, and a prominent opposer of apartheid. (Cambridge Jones/ Getty Images.)

> "The escalating resistance of black, Colored and Indian people is not given the prominence it deserves in undermining the apartheid system."

era of increased poverty, violence and crime. Moreover, all the neighboring states around South Africa were more or less dependent on South Africa for job opportunities, for electric power, for the use of ports and transport. Any action taken against South Africa which could adversely affect the economy would inevitably have repercussions in the neighboring states. This was why these countries, although demanding sanctions, continued to trade briskly with us.

It was true that many blacks in South Africa felt that economic sanctions were the only lever to pressure the government into making changes. In addition, some black leaders, such as Desmond Tutu, averred that "blacks were suffering so much already that a little more suffering caused by unemployment would not make any difference." I disagreed. There is no social security safety net in South Africa, no dole and no food stamps. Unemployment was a dire experience for vast numbers of workers not covered by the unemployment insurance fund. Maintenance of existing jobs and the creation of more jobs was the commitment of every candidate in the United States at election time. Why could this objective be disregarded in the case of South Africa? Survey after survey showed that the answer was "No" when the question "Do you approve of economic sanctions if your own job is in jeopardy?" was posed. The destruction of apartheid was not at issue; that was common cause. The issue was the strategy to be employed.

Certainly there was justification in the challenge by Tutu, that those who were against sanctions must suggest an alternative means of forcing the government to make necessary changes. My view was that it was economic growth which would empower black workers and give their trade unions the muscle to use the only effective weapon at their disposal—industrial action. This differed from economic sanctions because strikes, stayaways and boycotts could be abandoned or reversed when their objective had been obtained, whereas lost markets were not readily regained. When companies disinvested from South Africa, they invested elsewhere and were unlikely to rush back when the political climate had altered, as the Rhodesia/Zimbabwe experience demonstrated. . . .

Several Factors Played Roles in Change

The extent to which sanctions were responsible for the dismantling of apartheid is still a contentious issue. Those against sanctions, including myself, concede that sanctions expedited the process, but also are of the opinion that the claim of the pro-sanctions lobby—that the imposition of punitive measures was the major reason for [President F.W.] de Klerk's about-turn—ignores many factors.

One of them was the demise of communism in the USSR and Eastern Europe, which deprived the National Party government of its contention that it was the main bulwark against communism on the African continent. Thus the justification for arbitrary measures as a defense against the "total onslaught" of communism could no longer be used.

Another was that many major changes took place before the American Congress passed the Anti-Apartheid Act, with its widely ranging trade and other strictures, in November 1986, and before the European Community increased its sanctions against South Africa.

Finally, the escalating resistance of black, Colored and Indian people is not given the prominence it deserves in undermining the apartheid system.

But the argument about the efficacy of sanctions, disinvestment and divestment is now irrelevant to the task at hand. A high price was paid in economic terms by the thousands of people who lost their jobs in the labor-intensive sectors of the economy such as agriculture and coal mining, and in an area like Port Elizabeth, in the Eastern Cape, where economic devastation followed divestment by the American motor car companies. Recovery of the economy, the creation of jobs and the provision of housing and education must now be the priority considerations. And those countries, organizations and individuals that advocated punitive measures surely now have a major responsibility to encourage investment, to stimulate economic activity and to exert their influence to rescue South Africa from the poverty and violence engulfing the country. Inheriting a wasteland will not benefit any of the groups presently vying for power.

Truth and Reconciliation Set South Africa on a Path to Racial Healing

Alex Boraine

After serving as deputy chair of the Truth and Reconciliation Commission, Alex Boraine wrote a book about the group's work. In this excerpt, he considers the critics' positions and concludes that the commission made a great contribution toward establishing the truth, helping victims heal, and showing how the country should proceed. He asserts that a significant aspect of reconciliation involves bridging the gap between the poor and the wealthy. Boraine acknowledges that initial progress in postapartheid South Africa was slow and somewhat superficial, but he insists that those first steps have taken the country in the right direction.

Alex Boraine founded and has led the International Center for Transitional Justice. An ordained Methodist minister, he has been a member of the South African Parliament and a law professor in the United States.

SOURCE. Alex Boraine, *A Country Unmasked*. Cape Town, South Africa: Oxford University Press, 2000. Copyright © 2000 Alex Boraine. Reproduced by permission of Oxford University Press.

Many commentators who have commended the Truth and Reconciliation Commission have also criticised one particular aspect of its work. The criticism runs something like this: the Commission has certainly told some home truths and uncovered significant knowledge about our past, but it offers very little in the way of reconciliation.

Athol Jennings, the former director of Vuleka Trust, responding to a survey assessing the impact of the Commission, stated, 'The TRC has been good at revealing the truth. The reconciliation side of things appears to be almost an afterthought that was tagged on.' Gilbert A. Lewthwaite of the *Baltimore Sun*, reporting from Johannesburg, wrote, 'The Truth and Reconciliation Commission ends its investigation of this nation's past tomorrow, having produced horrifying truths and not much reconciliation.' R.W. Johnson, a very harsh critic

The Human Drama

Through novels and plays, a notable set of white South Africans created powerful attempts at reconciliation with their country's unique and painful truth.

The 1991 Nobel Prize for Literature went to Nadine Gordimer, whose father was Latvian and Jewish and whose mother's family was British. In short stories and novels—publication of which began in 1949—Gordimer wrote of love, betrayal, commitment, and prejudice among South Africans. The Nobel Prize address said: "Conveying to the reader a powerful sense of authenticity, and with wide human relevance, she makes visible the extremely complicated and utterly inhuman living conditions in the world of racial segregation."

Alan Paton's ethnicity was English and Scottish. His best-known book was his second, *Cry, the Beloved Country* (1948), which conveyed a plea for racial peace. He was prolific as a novelist, poet, and biographer until his death in 1988. He helped found the country's Liberal Party and worked for prison reform. The *Dictionary of Literary Biography* notes that Paton of the TRC since its inception, commented on the Commission soon after its final report was handed to President Mandela. In an article published in the *New York Times* he argued that 'The final report of South Africa's Truth and Reconciliation Commission—a 3000-page verdict

> Someone who has never come to terms with deep hurt and anger will be blighted by unresolved memories forever.

on the entire apartheid era that was released on Friday—appeared to have done something for truth but very little for reconciliation.' I was in New York at the time and when I read the column I wrote to the editor:

History will judge whether or not Johnson's criticism is accurate. It is, nevertheless, worth making two points in this regard. The first is that while truth may not always lead to reconciliation, there can be no genuine, lasting reconciliation without truth. Certainly lies, half-truths

was for decades "South Africa's most widely read novelist."

Athol Fugard, whose parents were English and Afrikaner, began writing plays in the 1950s. His breakthrough work is *Boesman and Lena*, first staged in 1969. It and *Master Harold . . . and the Boys* are among his plays that have been released as films as well. "Fugard's works are marked by an experientially driven search for truth and an attendant celebration of humanity," says *The Literary Encyclopedia*.

The 2003 Nobel Prize in Literature went to J.M. Coetzee, whose parents were English-speaking Afrikaners. He began writing fiction in 1969, and his books have included *In the Heart of the Country, Waiting for the Barbarians, Life & Times of Michael K*, and *Disgrace*. The Nobel Prize address said: "You are a Truth and Reconciliation Commission on your own. . . . You have dug deeply into the ground of the human condition with its cruelty and loneliness. You have given a voice to those outside the hierarchies of the mighty."

and denial are not a desirable foundation on which to build the new South Africa. Second, it is readily conceded that it is not possible for one commission, with a limited time-span and resources, on its own to achieve reconciliation against the background of decades of oppression, conflict and deep divisions. . . .

Revelations Make Change Possible

There are many who would argue that an achievement of the Commission was not to perpetuate the myth of the so-called rainbow nation where everyone claims to love one another, but to reveal the serious divide that does exist; the acknowledgement of this divide is the first step towards bridging it. It could be added that someone who has never come to terms with deep hurt and anger will be blighted by unresolved memories forever. I think the Commission can claim some credit for helping many to face up to the truth of the past, with all its horror and shame, not in order to dwell there but to deal with that past and move into a freer existence. Anger acknowledged can be as healing as the outpouring of suffering and grief. . . .

There can be little doubt that many of those who appeared before the Commission felt an enormous sense of relief, simply because they had an opportunity for the first time in their lives to tell their stories publicly and to regain their sense of human dignity. One such person was Lucas Sikwepere, who appeared before the Commission in Cape Town in 1996. He had to be led up to the platform because he was blind. He had been shot in the face by the police and had later been very badly tortured after becoming more politically active as a direct result of losing his sight. He told his story in some detail, and when asked if there

> Reconciliation, in [the view of one affected by the violence], involved the healing of perpetrators as well as victims.

Deputy Chairman of the Truth and Reconciliation Commission Alex Boraine, center, sits between South African President Nelson Mandela, left, and leader of the the right-wing Freedom Front, Constand Viljoen. (AP Images.)

was anything else he wanted to add he said, 'I feel what has been making me sick all the time is the fact that I couldn't tell my story. But now it feels like I got my sight back by coming here and telling you the story.'

Tim Ledgerwood, a former conscript in the South African Defence Force, alleged that he had been severely tortured by the security police. The process of telling his story to the Commission, he said, had deeply affected his life, because he now felt an enormous freedom to talk about his experiences to others as well. He said that he had been 'freed from a prison in which I have been for 18 years. It is also as if my family has been freed. . . . The silence is ending and we are waking up from a long bad nightmare.' . . .

Cynthia Ngewu, whose son was killed by the police in the infamous 'Guguletu Seven' incident, explained to the Commission that reconciliation, in her view,

> "Accepting coexistence is merely a step in what we should be working towards."

involved the healing of perpetrators as well as victims: 'What we are hoping for when we embrace the notion of reconciliation is that we restore the humanity to those who were perpetrators. We do not want to return evil by another evil. We simply want to ensure that the perpetrators are returned to humanity.' Ngewu was bereaved and deeply angry, but, remarkably, she thought not only of her own particular needs, which were great, but of the needs of the very people who killed her son. If this is not the beginning of reconciliation in a particular person as well as in a particular community then I don't know what is. . . .

Socioeconomic Progress Must Be Part of the Reconciliation Process

A particularly strong recommendation by the TRC was that

> Government accelerate the closing of the intolerable gap between the advantaged and disadvantaged in our society by, among other things, giving even more urgent attention to the transformation of education, the provision of shelter, access to clean water and health services and the creation of job opportunities. The recognition and protection of socio-economic rights are crucial to the development and the sustaining of a culture of respect for human rights.

The Commission went further and said that all South Africans should recognise that the public sector alone cannot bring about economic justice; the private sector has a major responsibility, and the Commission urged it to consider special initiatives in the form of a fund for training, empowerment, and opportunities for the disadvantaged and dispossessed in South Africa.

The Commission specifically recommended that

a scheme be put in place to enable those who benefited from apartheid policies to contribute towards the alleviation of poverty. In submissions made to the Commission a wealth tax was proposed. The Commission does not, however, seek to prescribe one or other strategy but recommends that urgent consideration be given by government to harnessing all available resources in the war against poverty.

In other words, the Commission recognised in public utterances and in its written report that reconciliation without economic justice is cheap and spurious. . . .

While many white people mouth platitudes about reconciliation without believing them, there are benefits to their changed behaviour. The farmer who pays his workers a better wage and provides improved working conditions and housing may not like what he is doing, but he accepts that it is necessary and therefore changes his behaviour. The way whites treat blacks in institutions, in shops, and on city streets is vastly different from what it was a few years ago. Their behaviour has changed for the better and has resulted in a commitment to coexistence, an almost unconscious recognition that we share the same space, the same country, and therefore we simply have to get on. But changed behaviour is not a deep, fundamental, religious experience of reconciliation. Accepting coexistence is merely a step in what we should be working towards: a deeper, more abiding, and more caring concern for each other as fellow South Africans and fellow human beings. But we must face up to the reality that in many cases it is not hearts that have changed but circumstances. . . .

I believe the TRC contributed to a national process of acknowledgement, accountability, and responsibility which has unlocked the greater possibility of a measure of reconciliation, not only for individuals, but also for the nation.

The Truth and Reconciliation Commission Fell Short

Anthea Jeffery

In the following selection, based on her book *The Truth About the Truth Commission*, Anthea Jeffery alleges that the Truth and Reconciliation Commission's own conclusions acknowledge how much it missed. For example, almost all of the 21,300 victim statements were unverified. She also questions the commission's logic and fairness, noting that it provided context for violence committed by the African National Congress but much less so for the government's violence or for violence committed by the ANC rival the Inkatha Freedom Party.

Anthea Jeffery, author of six books, is a special research consultant to the South African Institute of Race Relations.

SOURCE. Anthea Jeffery, "The Truth About the Truth Commission," *Human Rights*, vol. 27, Spring 2000, pp. 19–22. Copyright © 2000 American Bar Association. All rights reserved. Reproduced by permission of the author.

South Africa's Truth and Reconciliation Commission (TRC) was established in 1995 to foster reconciliation among South Africans by revealing the truth about the killings and other gross violations of human rights committed on all sides in the conflicts of the past. Its mandate period extended from March 1960 (the Sharpeville massacre) to May 1994 (Nelson Mandela's inauguration as president).

The TRC's founding legislation requires that it provide a factual, comprehensive, even-handed, and fully contextualized account of these gross violations. It mandates the TRC to identify the perpetrators of violations and hold them accountable. It also authorizes the TRC to grant amnesty to perpetrators on certain conditions, and to assist victims by, among other things, giving them a cathartic opportunity to relate their sufferings. . . .

On its publication in October 1998, the TRC's report was generally uncritically applauded. Careful evaluation shows, however, that the TRC deserves only a portion of its wide acclaim. It succeeded in capturing some of the horror perpetrated in the name of Apartheid and helped many victims come to terms with their suffering. However, its account of past conflict is fundamentally flawed by both the methods that it used and the aspects of violence that it left out.

> It is . . . questionable whether even 100 of its 21,300 victim statements could pass muster as 'factual evidence.'

The TRC's founding legislation makes clear the criteria by which the work of the TRC is to be evaluated, notably: (1) how factual was the evidence? (2) how comprehensive was it? (3) how objectively was it compiled and analyzed? and (4) how well was it contextualized? The TRC, as a statutory commission of inquiry, was also required to make "defensible findings according to established legal principles" and to base its findings on a "balance of probabilities." These requirements give rise

South African police remove the body of a black woman killed during the Sharpeville massacre. That incident, on March 21, 1960, later became the earliest to be placed within the Truth and Reconciliation Commission's authority. (Christie/Hulton Archive/Getty Images.)

to two additional questions: (1) were established legal principles applied? and (2) were the probabilities properly assessed?

The Victim and Amnesty Statements Are Questionable

The TRC received some 21,300 victim statements, detailing approximately 38,000 gross violations of human rights. Based on these statements, the TRC implied that it had a large, comprehensive, and reliable body of information at its disposal on which to ground its findings of accountability. This was not the case.

The majority of victim statements (about 19,200 or some 90 percent) were not given under oath, and few, if any, were tested under cross-examination. The TRC claimed to have corroborated all victim statements, but did so on a "low level" that excluded the key issue of perpetrator identity. It nevertheless used victim statements to make findings of accountability against named individuals and/or organizations. In about 17,500 instances, deponents gave second-hand accounts of violations experienced by others, many of which must have been based on hearsay rather than personal observation. It is thus questionable whether even 100 of its 21,300 victim statements could pass muster as "factual evidence."

Amnesty applications to the TRC totaled 7,127. Of these, some 1,340 dealt with gross violations and qualified for public hearing. However, at the time the TRC compiled its report, only 102 had been heard and confirmed as accurate by the granting of amnesty. At least 1,240 statements relating to gross violations had not yet been heard. The TRC thus reached its major conclusions about culpability for violence when some 90 percent of relevant amnesty statements had still to be considered.

The Findings Are Not Even-Handed

The TRC's statutory obligation was to provide as complete a picture as possible of the gross violations committed in the past. However, the TRC Report is far from comprehensive. Not only had it still to consider some 90 percent of relevant amnesty evidence (as noted above), but the amnesty statements it dealt with were not sufficiently representative. It received more amnesty applications from ANC [African National Congress] supporters than from any other group, but most of these were still unheard when it wrote its report.

Moreover, the killings for which it apportioned accountability (some 8,500) amounted to fewer than half the 20,500 political fatalities that occurred from 1984 to 1994 alone. These further killings have yet to be explained. . . .

The TRC was obliged to explain the motives and perspectives of perpetrators of gross violations, as well as any "antecedent factors" (such as prior provocation) that might have influenced them. It failed to do this in a consistent manner. It went to significant lengths to contextualize gross violations perpetrated by the ANC, explaining (for example) the circumstances in which ANC bombing operations had sometimes gone awry and killed civilians. By contrast, the TRC gave short shrift to the NP [the ruling National Party] perspective that normal legal processes were ineffective against revolutionary violence. It also failed to canvass adequately the question of prior provocation in relation to IFP [Inkatha Freedom Party, a rival of the ANC] attacks. The TRC's findings against the NP and the IFP would carry more weight if it had reflected their perspectives and given reasons for rejecting these.

The TRC acknowledged that it was obliged to make defensible findings on the basis of established legal principles. Such principles required, at a minimum, that it verify its evidence, take account of all relevant information, and uphold basic principles of justice including *audi alteram partem*. (*Audi alteram partem* is Latin for "hear the other side," and requires that an alleged perpetrator be given an opportunity to give his or her side of the story.) Such principles also required, as an essential safeguard against arbitrary decision making, the giving of reasons for findings made.

The TRC failed, however, to adhere to these requirements. In particular, it generally omitted to cite evidence or reasoning to substantiate its findings. . . .

The importance of truth in promoting reconciliation is frequently acknowledged by the TRC.

Only the entire and unvarnished truth, stressed the TRC, could provide a solid basis for reconciliation. "Narrow memories of past conflicts could too easily provide the mobilization for further conflicts," it warned, while "lies, half-truths and denial were not a desirable foundation on which to build the new South Africa."

The TRC was, thus, keenly aware of the importance of truth in promoting reconciliation. It implied that it had succeeded in excluding "lies, halftruths, and denial," and asserted that there could be little dispute about how "strong on truth" it had been.

These claims are questionable, at best. In fact, what the commission has done is to focus on only half the story and to tell that half in a selective and distorted way.

Mandela Displayed a Personal Version of Reconciliation

Patti Waldmeir

In the following selection, Patti Waldmeir reports specific examples of newly elected black president Nelson Mandela going out of his way, without reluctance or bitterness, to make personal contact with white people who had supported apartheid, including wives of leaders and ardent fans of the national rugby team. His support of the all-white rugby team in their quest for the World Cup, Waldmeir asserts, allowed white South Africans to regain their national pride and engaged the rest of the nation in a sport that previously symbolized white rule.

Journalist Patti Waldmeir was the *Financial Times'* chief correspondent in South Africa from 1989 to 1996, and she since has been the newspaper's U.S. editor and a columnist.

The huge black man in the brightly colored shirt beamed down at the tiny, white-haired lady dressed in pink. The frail ninety-four-year-old had just handed the elderly man a cup of tea and *koeksisters* [a traditional South African dessert]. Now she was preparing to read out a letter, written in her uncertain childlike hand, to thank him for coming.

Anxiously clutching the two-page missive, she became more and more upset as she found she could not read it without her glasses. The gentle black man peered over her shoulder and began softly prompting her in Afrikaans. The letter was addressed to State President Nelson Mandela. The signature at the bottom was that of Mrs. Betsie Verwoerd, widow of the architect of apartheid, Hendrik Verwoerd.

Mandela had gone to visit the widow Verwoerd at her retirement home in the empty vastness of the Northern Cape province, at the town of Orania. There, she lives with 460 other Afrikaners in a private colony where blacks are not allowed. . . . President Mandela visited her for the excellent reason that he was invited. He had asked Mrs. Verwoerd to take tea with him in Pretoria, but she declined on grounds of infirmity. So she wrote to thank him, and threw in a pro forma Afrikaans phrase of the "do drop in if you're ever in the neighborhood" variety. He took her up on it.

> Mandela vowed to dedicate the rest of his life to completing the unfinished business of liberation.

Soon, he was helping her read out a letter calling on him to "dispose of the fate of the Afrikaners with wisdom." When she had finished, she looked up to where he towered above her, with a radiant smile of thanks. She packed Mandela off to visit the statue of her husband that stands on a hill above the town. The new president commented that the statue looked very small. Verwoerd would cast no shadow in the land of Mandela.

The Mission Goes Beyond Apartheid's End

Hendrik Verwoerd decreed certain truths to be self-evident: that race was bondage; that ethnicity was fate. Nelson Mandela's mission was to set South Africa free from that color-coded prison.

That mission did not end on the day apartheid ceased to exist. Mandela vowed to dedicate the rest of his life to completing the unfinished business of liberation—the psychological, economic, and social emancipation of South Africa. He would preach his religion of non-racialism to all his countrymen. He would create prayerful symbols of a single nationhood, to unite the many peoples of South Africa in one rainbow. And he would tackle the toughest challenge of all: the battle for economic equality and prosperity, which would determine the fate of democracy itself. . . .

The will to reconcile had to come from the victors, and black South Africa readily supported Mandela's project. Africans are not a vengeful people; the guiding principle of their traditional culture is *ubuntu*, a concept only roughly translatable into English, but one that embodies charity, forgiveness, generosity, and an essential humanity. Archbishop Desmond Tutu, a great proponent of *ubuntu*, once explained it to me like this: "We say that a human being is a human being because he belongs to a community, and harmony is the essence of that community. So *ubuntu* actually demands that you forgive, because resentment and anger and desire for revenge undermine harmony. In our understanding, when someone doesn't forgive, we say that person does not have *ubuntu*. That is to say, he is not really human."

Wearing the national rugby team's cap, South African President Nelson Mandela shakes hands with Springbok team member Tiaan Strauss before the start of the 1995 World Cup games. (Gary Bernard/ AFP/Getty Images.)

> "Mandela chose rugby, high totem of Boer nationalism, to buttress his silver bridge."

Black Politicians Follow Mandela's Lead

Mandela made non-racialism the new civil religion of South Africa. He spoke of giving nervous minorities a "silver bridge to cross" to the new South Africa, and he began to trace its path from the moment he was elected.

The politics of reconciliation reigned supreme in those early days, and every ANC [African National Congress] politician did his bit to contribute. ANC provincial premiers went out of their way to speak Afrikaans, the hated "language of the oppressor," one of eleven new official languages. Ordinary people showed no desire to rock the boat: they left statues of Verwoerd and Vorster carefully on their pedestals, and street signs in place. The vast majority of politically inspired place names remained unchanged; when they were altered, neutral replacements were chosen. Reconciliation began to seem almost a cliché of the new South Africa.

Until Nelson Mandela discovered rugby.

With his deft feel for the politics of symbolism—and his total disdain for political correctness—Mandela chose rugby, high totem of Boer nationalism, to buttress his silver bridge. Rugby was a sport which apartheid's architects had embraced with a passion they reserved for nothing else but religion and politics. If the Dutch Reformed Church was the National Party at prayer, rugby was the National Party at play. For blacks, the sport came to symbolize the arrogance of Afrikaner power, and the brutality and aggression that went with it.

The Afrikaner government took the sport deadly seriously. In 1961, Verwoerd banned dark-skinned Maoris from the visiting New Zealand rugby team, sparking a process that led, more than twenty years later, to South Africa's expulsion from world rugby. For many Afrikaners, rugby isolation was the harshest cut of all: they could survive economic sanctions, the cultural boycott, the arms and oil embargoes, but they could not live without rugby. So the arrival of the world's top teams to contest the World Rugby Cup in South Africa in May 1995 was an occasion for white jubilation. Afrikaners had swopped apartheid for rugby, and there was every sign they thought it a fair deal.

Mandela Chooses a Stunning Symbol for Unity

Blacks ignored the event; they played soccer, not rugby. Apartheid had kept them separate, even in sport. Mandela could not accept that. He was the president of all South Africans, and he could not discriminate, in sport or in politics. Support for the national rugby team, the Springboks (the squad was all-white, after its lone coloured [mixed race] player was sidelined due to injury), was one of the patriotic requirements of citizenship in the new South Africa. Mandela, the first citizen, was going to make that point.

> Mandela fueled a national hysteria [for rugby] which transcended race.

He did so in spectacular fashion, turning up to celebrate the quintessential black public holiday, Sowetoday (which marks the 1976 massacre of schoolchildren in Soweto), wearing a green rugby supporter's cap, complete with the hated Springbok emblem, symbol of apartheid sport. "You see this cap I am wearing?" he asked his bemused supporters. "This cap does honor to our boys who are playing France" (in the World Cup semi-final). "I ask you to stand by them, because they are our kind," he said. Fifteen Afrikaner boys, raised on apartheid and drawn from the most conservative circles of Afrikanerdom. Finally, they were Africa's kin.

Over the week leading up to the June 24 final, Mandela fueled a national hysteria which transcended race. His boyish enthusiasm was infections as he visited the team on their practice fields and in their dressing rooms. He won the devotion of Springbok Captain François Pienaar, who said he would "play his heart out" for the president.

Then, as the team took the field for the final, Mandela emerged on the pitch wearing the green and gold, number 6 jersey of Captain Pienaar, and the overwhelmingly white crowd went wild. Afrikaans accents chanted, "Nelson, Nel-son," a sign of intimacy and approval that would have been unthinkable only days before. In the stands, thousands of white faces were painted with the garish colors of the new South African flag, and thousands of white hands waved it, acknowledging, for the first time, their loyalty to this most central symbol of the new nation. White Springbok lips stumbled through a rendi-

Mandela's Rival

For two decades, Nelson Mandela had a powerful competitor for the leadership of black interests in South Africa: Mangosuthu Buthelezi.

A chief of the Zulu tribe—historically the country's most powerful black ethnic group—Buthelezi became an activist in the African National Congress (ANC). But he split from the ANC in 1975 and led an organization known as Inkatha.

Buthelezi disagreed with the ANC's backing of guerrilla violence and global sanctions against South Africa. To end apartheid, he favored tribal independence. Clashes between Inkatha

and ANC supporters increased in the early 1990s. Later, a Truth and Reconciliation Commission report said Inkatha and white supremacists had collaborated in killing hundreds of people.

In the 1994 elections, the first all-races national balloting in the country, Buthelezi led Inkatha in challenges to Mandela's ANC. The Inkatha campaign emphasized autonomy for provinces, the rights of chiefs, hard work, and family values.

Remarkably, after winning the presidential election, Mandela appointed Buthelezi to his cabinet.

tion of the national anthem, *Nkosi sikeleli' Afrika*. White spectators bellowed out the new Springbok theme song, "Shosholoza," a traditional African work song that had become a favorite of the banned ANC in the 1980s. The cultural crossover was dizzying.

The "Bokke," as they were affectionately known, desperately wanted to win, and they did, after the almost intolerable excitement of extra time. Their victory proved to be the most potent political event since the release of Mandela. Nothing could compare with it—not the muted festivities of an exhausted electorate after the April 1994 elections; not the solemn emotionalism of the inauguration. This was pure, non-racial joy of a kind South Africa had never seen in 350 years of shared history. . . .

With Mandela's Help, Leaders' Wives Cross Boundaries

Mandela had not yet finished with his campaign to prove that, as he said in Afrikaans at his inauguration, "*Wat verby is verby*" ("What's done is done"). Again and again, his actions spoke of a triumph over bitterness. He built a retirement home identical to his prison bungalow. He was shown on South African television signing letters of congratulation to retiring members of the security forces, thanking them for their dedicated service—to the cause of suppressing the ANC.

He invited the wives of all South Africa's past political leaders, white and black, to lunch (this was the invitation Betsie Verwoerd had to decline). The widow of Steve Biko, the black-consciousness leader murdered by police in 1977, lunched with the widow of the prime minister in whose jail he died, John Vorster. Elize Botha, wife of [former prime minister] P.W., was seen helping Mrs. Urbania Mothopeng, widow of the former leader of the ultra-radical Pan Africanist Congress, to her feet in the presidential garden. Mandela complimented Mrs. Botha on her attire: she wore a black jacket bordered with the intricate beadwork of the Ndebele tribe, her own tribute to Africa. The widow of ANC leader Oliver Tambo exclaimed with delight on meeting Mrs. Botha, "I've seen you on TV!" Mandela said the gathering was "a practical way of forgetting the past."

Blacks Won Democracy but Not Justice

Nigel Gibson

In the following selection, Nigel Gibson criticizes the new South African government for giving a higher priority to business interests than to the working class—despite the new leaders' roots in black poverty. He asserts that the emphasis on free market capitalism over social movement politics has resulted in the continuation of the apartheid structure. In effect, Gibson says, the new structure unjustly blames the victims for being poor. An author and editor, Gibson is an expert in African studies. He teaches at Emerson College in Boston.

Why has so little changed in the seven years since the end of apartheid? South Africa remains a country of extremes, of great riches and great poverty, where the poor are still black and the rich predominantly white. How were the dreams of free-

SOURCE. Nigel Gibson, "Transition from Apartheid," *Journal of Asian & African Studies*, vol. 36, 2001, pp. 65–85. Copyright © 2001 by Journal of Asian & African Studies. Courtesy of Brill Academic Publishers.

> The neoliberal economic agenda has reinforced the highly unequal society inherited from apartheid.

dom and social and economic equality so quickly dashed? The answers are complicated and are partly a result of processes of depoliticization resulting from an elite model of transition. . . .

One key development in post-apartheid South Africa . . . is the transformation of an apparently radical opposition movement into a pro business group, advocating fiscal conservatism and free market capitalism. President Thabo Mbeki represents the foregrounding of business and technocratic interests in the ANC [African National Congress] who champion technology as an answer to the problem of national development. In other words, Mbeki's government represents the victory of technology over movement politics; that is to say, it represents the depoliticization of politics. . . .

Many on the South African left had articulated the hope of socialist democracy. Even the populist Freedom Charter spoke the language of direct participation and was tied to the idea of a structural change in the ownership of land—"all who work on it"—and in the control of factories—"by the people." Yet post-apartheid South Africa has abandoned these goals. The neoliberal economic agenda has reinforced the highly unequal society inherited from apartheid. But at the same time an oppositional political culture has not been allowed to develop. Instead, a whole layer of experienced organizers from civic organizations and trade unions have been seconded to government departments, thereby creating a significant loss of seasoned activists and helping to sow ideological confusion among the rank and file. . . .

The neoliberal shift has created more unemployment as well as an ideological justification for it. It has shifted the blame for poverty from the apartheid state to the free market, and thus onto the poor themselves, individualizing the process and obscuring the living legacy of the structural victims of apartheid. . . .

New Movements Could Challenge a Disappointing Present

As the rhetoric of the "national democratic struggle" dissipates into that of an "African Renaissance," new struggles will develop. The question is whether such movements can develop their own voices and develop a "higher conception of life," as [Marxist philosopher Antonio] Gramsci puts it, and whether intellectuals can hear the voices. The answer is far from clear. In post-apartheid South Africa the armed criminal gangs may be the only option for the unemployed young people. These gangs could easily become politicized and operate along the lines of a "lumpenproletariat" described by [revolutionary author Frantz] Fanon either as a revolutionary or counter revolutionary force. Movements will emerge, just as they continue to do around the world, articulating new needs and new goals, and the conditions in South Africa certainly cry out for them. . . . For all the sacrifice and struggle, the present seems a disappointment. This realization may engender a more critical thinking and, consequently, challenge intellectuals to develop new theoretical interventions and reflections and tap into the cerebral sediment in people's experiences. The struggle over the production of the past includes the recover of radical democratic ideas and experiments in the people's struggle for a new way of life. . . .

South African blacks experienced dramatically unequal conditions such as in this squatter camp within view of downtown Johannesburg. (AP Images.)

Are the problems of post-apartheid South Africa unique or do they repeat those of other African independence movements, which, upon taking over power, were unable to extricate themselves from the structures and discourses of the old regime? Did the South African anti-apartheid elite have a choice? Did it jump into a home-grown structural adjustment or was it pushed away from a genuine redistribution that would attempt to rebalance and redraw the social and economic map of apartheid?

The negotiated settlement provided the framework for continued "white privilege," which has been made all the more hegemonic through the development of a black middle class. Perhaps then South Africa provides the best opportunity, against Fanon's predictions that it was impossible, to see the development of a "productive" African bourgeoisie. Yet the social cost of creating this small middle class, without any guarantee of benefit, will be high, and the legacies of apartheid, on which it is built, perhaps higher.

Some Afrikaners Refuse to Go Along with Black Majority Rule

Martin Schönteich and Henri Boshoff

In a whites-only 1992 referendum in South Africa on whether the country should move toward sharing power with parties of other races, about a third voted "no." In the following selection, the authors outline how a hard-line movement on the losing side leaned toward a separate homeland for whites—by large-scale violence if necessary. But a widely publicized fatal incident in the spring of 1994, between members of a white-right organization and troops and civilians in a black homeland, undermined the efforts of the white right to take back control of South Africa. Martin Schönteich, a former prosecutor in the South African Department of Justice, is a senior researcher in crime, justice, and race relations. Henri Boshoff, also a South African, is a military and security expert.

SOURCE. Martin Schönteich and Henri Boshoff, *'Volk', Faith and the Fatherland: The Security Threat Posed by the White Right (Monograph No. 81)*. New Muckleneuk, Tshwane (Pretoria): Institute for Security Studies, 2003. Copyright © 2006–2009 Institute for Security Studies. All rights reserved. Reproduced by permission. www.issafrica.org.

The emergence of the contemporary extreme white right must be understood against the background of the rise of Afrikaner nationalism, and the divisions that have plagued Afrikanerdom for over a century. Moreover, that throughout their history Afrikaner nationalists tended to believe that the only way to confirm and protect the status and identity of the Afrikaner, and to prevent the group from being dominated by other ethnic groups or races, was to exercise power through self-determination in an ethnically homogenous territory.

The Anglo-Boer War (1899–1902) was an event of great consequence in Afrikaner right wing mythology. The courageous manner in which the outnumbered Republican Boers fought the war against the might of the British Empire, the suffering of non-combatants in British concentration camps (leading to the death of some 28,000 Boer women and children), the aggressive post-war Anglicisation policy, and the resultant poverty and loss of freedom, left an indelible mark on the national consciousness of the Afrikaner. Moreover, the guerrilla war which the Boers fought with considerable success against the British created popular heroes still revered by right wing Afrikaners today.

Towards the end of the Anglo-Boer War deep divisions developed among the Boers between the *bittereinders* (literally die-hards; those who fought to the bitter end) and the *hensoppers* (those who surrendered prematurely), over whether or not to continue the war. . . . A related theme derived from the war is that of treachery, used in this context to describe the behaviour of any member of the Afrikaner people who is deemed to have turned his back on his people. . . .

Many Whites Vote "No" to Sharing Power

In 1992 a referendum was held among whites about whether they supported the reform process of the

National Party government, which was leading to a power-sharing arrangement between the different race groups at central government level. The pro-reform, or "Yes" campaign, received the full backing of the liberal opposition Democratic Party, the media, the international community and the vast majority of commercial institutions and organised business in South Africa. . . .

> The mainstream white right began to seriously consider the idea of using force and violence on a large and organised scale.

Nevertheless, some 876,000 white South Africans voted against the reform process (31%). Again there were strong regional differences, with around half of votes cast in large parts of the Transvaal and Orange Free State voting "No." For example, in the Transvaal regions of Roodepoort, Kroonstad and Pietersburg (now Polokwane) 46% or more of the voters registered their opposition to the reform process.

After the white right's referendum defeat, the CP [Conservative Party] shifted its focus from winning control of the ballot box to a less ambitious goal, the attainment of Afrikaner self-determination in a sovereign Afrikaner, white homeland.

It was only after the referendum defeat, and the knowledge that another whites-only election was unlikely, that the mainstream white right began to seriously consider the idea of using force and violence on a large and organised scale to place pressure on the government to concede to their key demand of Afrikaner self-determination. . . .

After the referendum the CP informally dropped its position that the whole of apartheid South Africa should be restored to white rule. The party began drawing up boundaries for a smaller Afrikaner, white state which would include the then Western Transvaal (North West province), including Pretoria, the Orange Free State, and the Northern Cape province. The party was,

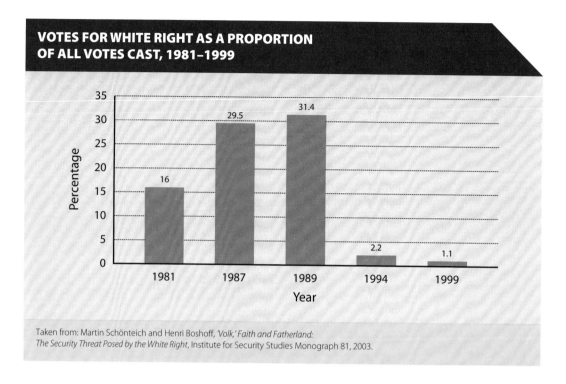

VOTES FOR WHITE RIGHT AS A PROPORTION OF ALL VOTES CAST, 1981–1999

Taken from: Martin Schönteich and Henri Boshoff, 'Volk,' Faith and Fatherland: The Security Threat Posed by the White Right, Institute for Security Studies Monograph 81, 2003.

however, split on whether such a partition plan should be negotiated with other parties through participation at the ongoing all-party talks taking place at the time. For many in the CP it was anathema to negotiate with the African National Congress (ANC), which most CP supporters regarded as a "communist-inspired terrorist movement." . . .

Right-Wing Whites Join with Conservative Blacks

In late 1992 the CP founded the Concerned South African Group (Cosag) in conjunction with other smaller white right wing movements, and three conservative black "homeland" leaders: Mangosuthu Buthelezi of KwaZulu, Lucas Mangope of Bophuthatswana and Oupa Gqozo of the Ciskei. As a multi-racial right wing alliance, Cosag sought to counter bilateral negotiations between the ANC and the National Party, and promoted the idea of a South African confederacy along largely ethnic lines.

In May 1993 the CP came together with 20 other white right wing groups and formed the Afrikaner Volksfront or AVF (Afrikaner People's Front), with the goal of promoting right wing unity and the realisation of an Afrikaner *volkstaat* (people's state). In July 1993, the AVF joined Cosag, and the latter was renamed the Freedom Alliance.

> "The Afrikaner people must prepare to defend themselves. A bloody conflict which will require sacrifices is inevitable."

The leader of the AVF was General Constand Viljoen, retired head of the South African Defence Force (SADF). [According to author J. Van Rooyen], with his impressive military record Viljoen commanded the "respect and loyalty not only of the more threatening of the paramilitary forces of the Right (including over fifty retired security force generals) but also of sections of the South African Defence Force". The fact that in addition to Viljoen, the AVF was led by a number of former security force generals gave new impetus to the scope and prospect of violent resistance by the white right.

The AVF rapidly mobilised widespread support among the white right. According to Viljoen, within six weeks of the AVF's founding the organisation had enrolled 150,000 members, many of whom had [in the words of author P. Stiff] "expressed their willingness to take up arms in support of the AVF". Viljoen initially declined to get involved in organising the white right to resist, by violence if necessary, the impending end of white rule. By mid-1993 Viljoen's views had changed, however:

> The Afrikaner people must prepare to defend themselves. A bloody conflict which will require sacrifices is inevitable, but we will gladly sacrifice because our cause is just. . . .

Resistance Takes the Country to the Edge of War

During the latter half of 1993 the AVF focused on preparing its members for armed resistance in the event of an ANC takeover of the whole South Africa. In such an event the AVF planned, with the help of sympathetic SADF and police units, to proclaim and defend an independent Afrikaner state in parts of the Transvaal and Orange Free State. Members of the AVF—and more specifically the Boere Krisisaksie—engaged in acts of sabotage in various parts of the country to place pressure on the country's constitutional negotiators to comply with the white right's demands for territorial autonomy in parts of South Africa. By early 1994 South Africa appeared to be at the precipice of a civil war, and serious analysts argued the white right potentially had the power to break up South Africa. . . .

In the run up to the 1994 election a state of emergency was declared in the Western Transvaal (North West province). This was done to counter an elaborate AVF-sponsored plan to establish an independent Boer state in a large part of the then Transvaal. The plan focused around some 50 towns and included the stockpiling of armoured vehicles and ammunition. Most of these towns were controlled by right wing councils, and many had awarded the AWB [Afrikaner Resistance Movement] and other right wing organisations the "freedom of the town". It was the first time that a state of emergency had been declared in South Africa in response to white political activity.

> The wounded AWB [Afrikaner Resistance Movement] occupants of the vehicle were executed at point-blank range by a black member of the BDF [Bophuthatswana Defense Force].

In what was to be a turning point for the white right, the AVF unsuccessfully attempted to support the ailing black "homeland" government of Bophuthatswana in

A member of a white-supremacist Afrikaner Resistance Movement (AWB) holds the group's flag as black South Africans walk past in Potchefstroom. (Alexander Joe/AFP/Getty Images.)

March 1994. ANC supporters in Bophuthatswana protested the "homeland" government's decision not to take part in the forthcoming election. In places the protests escalated into strike action by civil servants, rioting and widespread looting. Fearing that he would lose control over his "country", the president of Bophuthatswana, Lucas Mangope, asked a fellow Freedom Front ally, Constand Viljoen, for assistance. In response Viljoen mobilised some 1,500 AVF members who assembled outside of the Bophuthatswana capital of Mmabatho, where they were issued with Bophuthatswana Defence Force (BDF) rifles. At the same time about 500 members of the AWB also entered Bophuthatswana. . . .

Some of the AWB members went on the rampage, firing at BDF troops and civilians in Mmabatho. (This version of events is disputed by the AWB.) In response the BDF fired on an AWB vehicle. With its driver critically injured the vehicle came to a standstill. In front of rolling television cameras the wounded AWB occupants of the vehicle were executed at point-blank range by a black member of the BDF. Moreover, as a result of the AWB's actions, even Mangope loyalists turned against the "white invaders" and large sections of the BDF threatened to mutiny. Mangope ordered Viljoen to withdraw his supporters from Bophuthatswana, a request with which Viljoen complied.

The events in Bophuthatswana were to be the white right's undoing. The perception the extreme right had cultivated, that it was invincible, was shattered as South African television viewers witnessed the execution of two AWB members by a black man. This one event arguably dealt a decisive blow to the morale of the rank and file of the white right throughout the country. The fact that the AWB entered Bophuthatswana separately from the AVF members mobilised by Viljoen, and refused to fall under Viljoen's command, also revealed fundamental weaknesses and divisions in the white right's military preparedness for armed resistance.

For Viljoen and his followers the events in Bophuthatswana were a turning point. Viljoen felt that sections of the white right were too undisciplined, and the white right too divided, to shape it into a credible and effective fighting force. As a result Viljoen abandoned his plan of violent resistance to establish an Afrikaner state by force of arms.

Postapartheid Progress Has Been Significant but Not Sufficient

Richard Crockett

In the following selection, Richard Crockett finds that, a dozen years after the formal end of apartheid, the new government has made considerable economic progress, building new homes and providing millions of households with electricity and running water. Crockett points out, however, that many of the positive developments in South Africa have come from the creative efforts of the people rather than from government programs. Furthermore, Crockett asserts that the pace of change has been too slow, and the core supporters of the African National Congress (ANC) are impatient for real change. Crockett is a writer for *The Economist*, a weekly publication covering international news.

SOURCE. Richard Crockett, "Chasing the Rainbow," *The Economist*, vol. 378, April 8, 2006, pp. 3–5. Copyright © 2006 The Economist Newspaper Group. Reproduced by permission.

In the 12 years since the African National Congress (ANC) party triumphantly took power in South Africa's first multiracial democratic election, there have been plenty of reasons to be disappointed, even disillusioned, with Africa. The "aid darlings" of the West have come and gone. Yoweri Museveni of Uganda changed his constitution to win a third presidential term in dubious circumstances, and Meles Zenawi, Ethiopia's prime minister, ruined his reputation when his police shot dead scores of opposition supporters last year. Robert Mugabe, the last of the original "big men" of Africa, seems bent on impoverishing what was once one of the continent's most prosperous countries, and the government of Sudan continues with its genocidal military campaigns against its own people. Nor has the continent yet conquered famine: in the Horn of Africa, parts of Kenya, Somalia and Ethiopia are currently facing critical food shortages.

The Country Did Better Than Most

But through all this, South Africa has plotted its own course to relative stability, democracy and prosperity. It has even been trying to nudge the rest of Africa towards emulating its own success. In that sense, South Africa is beginning to lead the continent in an entirely new way.

> The cars rush through miles of shanty towns and townships on the Cape Flats, the geography of apartheid very much intact.

When the apartheid regime fell apart in 1990, South Africa, remarkably, did not erupt in flames. That it did not was due largely to the leadership of Nelson Mandela. No less remarkable since then has been the ANC's relentless campaign to alleviate the poverty and degradation of the victims of apartheid without resorting to counterproductive populism. Despite inheriting an economic mess from the outgoing National Party in 1994, the post-apartheid government has managed to

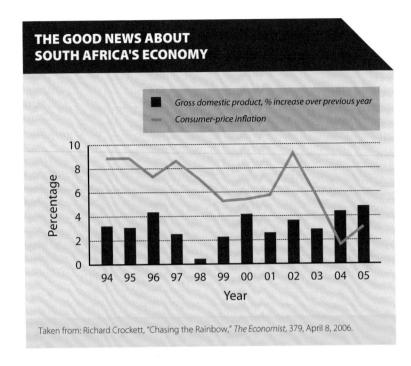

THE GOOD NEWS ABOUT SOUTH AFRICA'S ECONOMY

- ■ Gross domestic product, % increase over previous year
- Consumer-price inflation

Taken from: Richard Crockett, "Chasing the Rainbow," *The Economist*, 379, April 8, 2006.

These graphs show some positive economic trends in South Africa. The line graph shows a relatively low consumer price inflation. The bar graph shows a steady increase in gross domestic product.

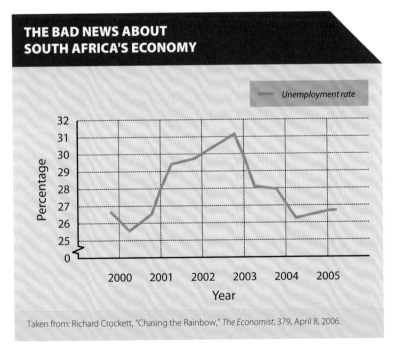

THE BAD NEWS ABOUT SOUTH AFRICA'S ECONOMY

- Unemployment rate

Taken from: Richard Crockett, "Chasing the Rainbow," *The Economist*, 379, April 8, 2006.

This graph indicates the high unemployment rate in South Africa, 2000–2005.

build 1.9 million new homes, connect 4.5 million households to electricity and provide 11 million homes with running water. Its targets for raising the living standards of its people are the most ambitious on the continent.

The People Are Impatient for More Progress

Yet a drive from Cape Town airport into the city's almost exclusively white suburbs at the foot of Table Mountain demonstrates that South Africa is still deeply scarred by the legacy of apartheid. Here the cars rush through miles of shanty towns and townships on the Cape Flats, the geography of apartheid very much intact. It is a similar story throughout South Africa. Yes, the shacks in Cape Town now have electricity. But what else has really changed? Yes, the giant township of Soweto, flashpoint of apartheid, now also has electricity and smart paved roads. But has its upgrading not further entrenched the separation of 3 million blacks from the city of Johannesburg, from which many were forcibly removed 50 years ago?

> Little of this [economic] growth has benefited [the ANC's] own core supporters, who are overwhelmingly poor and black.

There is now a sense of impatience over the pace of change in South Africa. For many, the country's advance towards Mr. Mandela's vision of a "rainbow nation" has slowed to a crawl. The government is well aware of this, and is now intervening in more and more areas of national life to try to speed up change.

Yet those interventions could do more harm than good. . . . South Africa has some good stories to tell about change, but few of them are entirely the ANC's doing. From education to foreign policy to crime-fighting, the South African people have found creative solutions to many of their problems. That creativity is South Africa's most impressive asset, and increasingly comes from the poorest and historically most disadvantaged of South Africa's communities, who are now building their own ladders out of poverty.

Economic Progress Has Not Benefited the Poorest South Africans

By rights, the government should be basking in the glow of an outstandingly successful economic performance over the past decade. Having inherited a pile of trouble from the disintegrating apartheid government, the government has since presided over an impressive 87 straight months of growth [as of spring 2006] (currently running at about 5% a year), low budget deficits and low inflation. . . .

Yet for all the good economic news, the government is looking politically more vulnerable than at any time since 1994, for a simple reason: little of this growth has benefited its own core supporters, who are overwhelmingly poor and black. . . . The problem is summed up by

Protesters draw fire from South African police in Cape Town, demanding housing and services from the African National Congress local government. (**AP Images.**)

the unemployment rate, which even on the narrowest official definition stands at about 27%, a slight increase on a year earlier, despite the 5% GDP growth. The economy is generating jobs, but not enough to keep pace with the number of new entrants into the labour market.

The government's other big problem is rising inequality. There is a lot of talk about a growing black middle class, but the number of people living on the poverty line may actually be rising. Thabo Mbeki, the country's president, has spoken of the gaping divide between South Africa's "first economy" and "second economy." . . .

The ANC has always pledged itself to work for the poor and the disadvantaged, so its grassroots supporters are particularly unhappy. Their discontent surfaced in the local elections on March 1st [2006], at which the ANC faced a genuine challenge for the first time in its brief democratic history. It did better than expected, but still saw its vote fall in some areas. Last year [2005], in the absence of any elections, there were about 880 illegal street protests, mostly about the lack of basic services and housing.

South Africa Needs Better Leadership in the Twenty-First Century

Marco MacFarlane

In the following selection from South Africa's leading policy research organization, Marco MacFarlane says the African National Congress is having a harder time governing than it did opposing apartheid. He finds the country leaderless and directionless, criticizing the government for being out of touch and inept. MacFarlane is the head of research at the South African Institute of Race Relations.

Under apartheid, the objective was clear: overthrow the oppressive regime. We had an enemy, an opponent that we could rail against and eventually overthrow. This enemy gave us direction and

SOURCE. Marco MacFarlane, "Look on My Works, Ye Mighty, and Despair!" *South African Institute of Race Relations*, May 30, 2008. Copyright © 2008 South African Institute of Race Relations. Reproduced by permission.

> The ANC has shown that it was not equal to the task . . . a task that involves hard work, quiet commitment, decisive action, and very few grand speeches.

purpose, and with its death, South Africans who had fought for so long against so much could finally be at peace. But then the realisation began to dawn that while apartheid lay dead at our feet, the results of decades of oppression were still alive. Post-apartheid leaders no longer needed to make grand speeches and lead fervent youths on marches. Instead the real work of nation building needed to begin.

Perhaps our leaders were unprepared for what the reversal of apartheid would entail. Certainly the ANC [African National Congress] has shown that it was not equal to the task. It was, and still is, a task that involves hard work, quiet commitment, decisive action, and very few grand speeches. Meetings and planning sessions and commissions and *lekgotlas* [debates or conversations] and discussion groups and *imbizos* [policy discussions] and committees et al. are not even the beginning of what is required in South Africa. We have plans and charters for almost every conceivable aspect of our socio-economic lives, but we have witnessed very few actions to back up those plans.

For a time, the government could perhaps be forgiven for its sluggish movement and tremulous voice. The problems that faced the post-apartheid state were enormous, and a well thought out plan was essential in tackling those problems. Evidence continues to mount, however, that somewhere along the way any sense of real purpose was lost. In a country that was world renowned for reconciliation, our political leaders decided to buy arms. With [the AIDS] pandemic sweeping through the nation, politicians decided that science was wrong and that crackpot theories also deserved a fair run. Having created a social welfare system that is often the only thing between the poor and starvation, our civil servants have

busied themselves with stealing grants. . . . As our neighbour's state [Zimbabwe] has fallen into ruin, a policy of diplomacy has been followed that was so quiet that it amounted to less than a whisper.

The Good Feeling of Liberation Is Now Exhausted

We are leaderless and directionless. Our commander in chief is so out of touch with the region that his statements become sound bites for caricaturists: Crime? What crime? AIDS? What AIDS? Crisis? What crisis?

The post-1994 euphoria has well and truly worn off, and South Africa finds itself in a position where the fundamentals have been ignored for far too long. The nation was told in a white paper in 1998 that the electricity

Activists protest the firing of Nozizwe Madlala-Routledge, South Africa's former deputy minister of health. President Thabo Mbeki fired the deputy minister for making an unauthorized trip to an AIDS conference. (**AP Images.**)

> Our idle elite continue to abdicate all responsibility for their failures.

supply would be insufficient by 2007. At the end of 2007 when the lights went out, nobody except the government was taken by surprise. We have known for more than a decade that our telecommunications regime is a huge impediment to growth, but still Telkom is effectively a monopoly. Public healthcare is in freefall, but our minister [cabinet member] is concerned with the state of the well-functioning private sector. The list of fundamental errors and omissions goes on.

The ANC cannot trade on its "liberation" status forever. Apartheid left our new democracy with a slew of problems, but the continued bungling of our politicians has failed to address most of them, and indeed has created many that were not there before. There has been no leadership in the AIDS crisis, unless we count misdirection as such. Corruption and graft are now endemic, and our re-racialised legislative environment only serves to deepen the problem. The energy crisis, predicted yet ignored for so long, is now showing its effects on our economy as growth slows and inflation soars. The list goes on, and our idle elite continue to abdicate all responsibility for their failures. Commended when they should be condemned, our politicians lurch from ill conceived plan to ill conceived action. South Africa and its people deserve better. Emerging from a dark history, this country requires selfless leaders whose discipline and commitment is unquestionable. Those leaders, it seems, have yet to show themselves.

The New Black Leadership Is Falling Short

Moeletsi Mbeki

Writing at the time his brother, Thabo Mbeki, was being forced out as president, Moeletsi Mbeki says in the following selection that South African government leaders have perpetuated inequalities. They substantially helped elite business interests, he asserts, while doling out humiliating small grants to poor black people. Moeletsi Mbeki is a business entrepreneur, political commentator, and deputy chairman of the South African Institute of International Affairs, an independent think tank in Johannesburg, South Africa.

The conference of the African National Congress [ANC] that was held last month [December 2007] was billed as a heavyweight contest between the party's president, Thabo Mbeki, and its deputy president,

SOURCE. Moeletsi Mbeki, "The Curse of South Africa," *New Statesman*, vol. 137, January 21, 2008, pp. 28–30. Copyright © 2008 New Statesman, Ltd. Reproduced by permission.

On September 21, 2008, the day the South African government went into emergency session to try to limit the political and economic fallout from his ouster, President Thabo Mbeki gets ready to address his cabinet in Pretoria. (AP Images.)

Jacob Zuma. The conference turned out to be much more than that. It was a complete rout, not only of the president, but also of his cabinet, the sitting national executive committee, and of Mbeki's economy team.

The December conference saw the ANC swing from the centre towards the left, if one believes the rhetoric. Jacob Zuma, the new president of the ANC, mobilised the support of the Congress of South African Trade Unions (Cosatu) and the South African Communist Party (SACP) in order to fight for leadership of the ANC.

The ANC is caught in a quandary. On the one hand, its members and leaders want to preserve the economic system inherited from the apartheid era so that they, too, can benefit from it through, for example, Black Economic Empowerment (an affirmative-action programme, initially designed by South Africa's big corporations, that favours the new black elite) and social grants from the government aimed at alleviating poverty. On the other hand, they hanker for change that will ameliorate the growing inequalities and pauperisation among black South Africans. They blame individuals within the organisation for not bringing about the socio-economic changes they would like to see, but do not dare to initiate themselves.

Much of the impetus behind the emerging instability in the ANC, however, is financial rather than ideological. The only solution would be for a leadership to emerge, from either within or outside the ANC, that has meaningful policies for building a more inclusive society in South Africa. Black Economic Empowerment and social welfare programmes do not fundamentally lead to such social inclusiveness. If anything, they entrench the inequalities inherited from the past and exacerbate new inequalities among the blacks.

The President Was Out of Touch

The undoing of President Mbeki and his cabinet was that they failed to understand that, with Zuma's rise, a new phenomenon of populism had entered the ANC. They also failed to understand the potential of populism to appeal to the black working class, the black poor in general, and a wide array of disgruntled people associated with the ANC who felt excluded from the inside track.

Their mistake was to see Zuma as a paranoiac who didn't deserve to be taken seriously. Mbeki compounded this error by standing against the populist Zuma but refusing to engage with him in public debate. He thereby appeared to be afraid of Zuma. This encouraged Zuma and his supporters to press ahead with their campaign and, paradoxically, Mbeki's silence persuaded many ANC members that Zuma's claim of persecution was valid.

Diamonds and Gold Can Be a Curse

South Africa is able to undertake both Black Economic Empowerment and large social welfare expenditures because of its vast natural resources, which are now selling at a premium due to the rapid industrialisation of the large countries of Asia. South Africa's fabulous mineral wealth has been seen as a blessing since the discovery of diamonds and gold in the 19th century. What gets overlooked is the curse that goes with vast natural-resource endowment.

Since the current commodities boom started in the late 1990s, the ANC government has been ratcheting up public spending on the welfare of the poor. Why? Out of the goodness of its heart, reply ANC leaders. Not so, say doubters: rather to placate the poor so that they do not rebel, but most importantly to buy their vote.

> Are South Africa's poor happy and grateful to the ANC government?

In his address to the ANC conference, President Mbeki went to great lengths to explain the good things the ANC government has done for South Africa's poor. He noted that the number of South Africans living below the poverty line fell from 51.4 percent in 2001 to 43.2 percent in 2006 and that the number of people receiving social grants increased from 2.6 million in 1999 to more than 12 million in 2006.

But are South Africa's poor happy and grateful to the ANC government? In theory they should be, given the largesse they are receiving. But judging by the support that Zuma and his communist and trade union allies have been able to mobilise among the poor against the mainstream ANC which runs the government, it appears South Africa's poor are very far from happy. This is where the resource curse comes in.

A country develops when it is able to harness the energies of its people and put them to productive use. There are, of course, exceptions to this rule. Oil-producing countries are one. For very little effort, petroleum-producing countries pump crude oil from the ground and sell it for fabulous prices to foreigners.

South Africa is similar to oil-producing countries in that it, too, has natural resources—gold, platinum, diamonds, coal, iron ore, and so on that are valuable to foreigners, who are willing to pay South Africa top dollar for them. While it takes more people to dig out South Africa's

> Governments of resource-rich countries think their people need not work and will be happy living off social grants.

minerals compared to those employed to pump up crude oil, mining is still a small employer. Despite employing very few people, mining, however, makes a huge contribution to the country's wealth, in that it accounts for more than half of export earnings. The value that the few people employed in mining produce far exceeds their income. The government, therefore, has large revenues from mining activity that it can redistribute to the rest of society that does not work in the mines. This is what is called a resource curse. Governments of resource-rich countries think their people need not work and will be happy living off social grants.

Government Aid Makes the Recipients Anxious

That is precisely the trap into which the ANC government has fallen. At least a quarter of the South African population receives social grants that would not be possible if South Africa were not mineral-rich. Without mineral wealth to redistribute, the government would have to work harder and be more creative to find solutions to unemployment and poverty.

Resource wealth makes it possible for the government not to have to put an effort into redeveloping the economy to create more jobs, and instead it sustains the unemployed and their dependents with social grants.

But do such grants make people happy as the ANC government expects? Paradoxically, while social grants contribute to putting food on the table, at a broader

> *The rest of society stigmatises [social grant] recipients as idle, worthless and parasitic.*

level they make the recipients more insecure because they do not know when the government will withdraw or reduce the size of their grants. Second, the grants accentuate the humiliation that unemployed people feel from being dependent and unable to look after themselves and their families. Every time they collect their social grants, recipients are subjected to all manner of humiliations by the government officials who administer the system. The rest of society stigmatises recipients as idle, worthless and parasitic.

What do South Africa's subsidised and marginalised people do to regain their self-respect? They support demagogues who claim that they, too, are marginalised, and therefore want to replace the ruling elites with people-friendly governments. This, in a nutshell, is what happened at the ANC conference and in the months leading up to it.

The African National Congress Has Achieved Much and Is Facing the Challenges

The National Executive Committee of the African National Congress

This excerpt from a major statement by South Africa's governing party in 2008 speaks of both successes and needs. One of the cited needs is equality for women. The statement marks achievements in the economy and lays out the challenges in addressing poverty, inequality, education, and public health.

The African National Congress was founded in 1912 with the stated aim of bringing all Africans together to defend their rights and freedoms.

SOURCE. The National Executive Committee of the African National Congress, "Statement of the National Executive Committee of the African National Congress on the Occasion of the 96th Anniversary of the ANC, January 8, 2008," *African National Congress*, January 8, 2008. Reproduced by permission.

On January 8th 2008, the African National Congress [ANC] celebrated its 96th anniversary, marking nearly a century of proud and tireless struggle to advance the cause of freedom for all our people.

This occasion provides an opportunity to reflect on the achievements of this great movement as it has worked, together with the masses, first to defeat the apartheid system, and then to vanquish the legacy of racial oppression and gender inequality.

It provides an opportunity to recall the heroic and selfless acts of countless South Africans who, over several decades, fought with determination and principle for peace, democracy and human and people's rights. They remain an example and inspiration to successive generations of freedom fighters as they grapple with the challenges of a changing terrain of struggle. We salute them today, these giants of our revolution, for what they have contributed to our nation and for the legacy they have left behind.

As is customary, this anniversary also provides an opportunity to reflect on the challenges of the moment, and to outline the tasks that the organisation must necessarily undertake to advance the historic mission of the African National Congress.

> All ANC structures will have a minimum of 50 percent representation of women.

The Party's Priorities Include Confronting Sexism

We undertake this important work having benefited from the deliberations and decisions of the 52nd ANC National Conference, held just a few weeks ago in Polokwane. This historic gathering of the highest structure of our movement adopted the policy and programme of the ANC for the next five years, providing a clear guide to all our structures, cadres and deployees. . . .

The decision by Conference to adopt a policy of gender parity within all structures of the movement has served to deepen our efforts to confront sexism, gender inequality and discrimination. Beginning with the NEC [National Executive Committee], all ANC structures will have a minimum of 50 percent representation of women.

We salute the membership of the ANC for continuing to provide leadership in the struggle for gender equality, serving as not only an example to broader South African society, but also providing an example of international best practice.

This decision is recognition that patriarchy will only be defeated through conscious, resolute and consistent action by men and women alike.

We are reminded at this moment of the words of the late ANC President, Comrade O.R. Tambo, when he said in 1981:

> Women in the ANC should stop behaving as if there was no place for them above the level of certain categories of involvement. They have a duty to liberate us men from antique concepts and attitudes about the place and role of women in society and in the development and direction of our revolutionary struggle.

This Conference decision is a response to the challenge O.R. Tambo put before the women and men of the ANC over 20 years ago. This decision is not the end of the struggle for the emancipation of women. Rather it is a springboard for a concerted, all-round effort to tackle sexism in all its forms and manifestations. . . .

Economic Progress Has Been Substantial

As we noted in Polokwane, we have made substantial progress since 1994 in transforming the economy to benefit the majority.

We have created conditions for the longest expansion of the South African economy in recorded history; the rate of growth averaging over 4.5% every year since 2004. Though still high, unemployment has begun to decline.

> We must make the creation of decent work opportunities the primary focus of our economic policies.

Since 2004, the number of employed people has been increasing by about half a million each year. This, together with the extension of social security and basic infrastructure and the distribution of assets to the poor, has led to a significant reduction in the level of severe poverty and improvements in the quality of life for millions of our people.

Improved macroeconomic conditions, reduced government debt and improved revenue collection has meant that greater resources are available for social and investment programmes, providing an opportunity, among other things, for a massive public sector infrastructure programme.

More Progress Is Necessary

However, serious challenges of unemployment, poverty and inequality remain.

Answering these challenges means that we must simultaneously accelerate economic growth and transform the quality of that growth. Conference said:

> Our most effective weapon in the campaign against poverty is the creation of decent work. Moreover, the challenges of poverty and inequality require that accelerated growth takes place in the context of an effective strategy of redistribution. . . .

During the course of this year, we must make the creation of decent work opportunities the primary focus of our economic policies. We need to make maximum

Photo on next page: The African National Congress party's Deputy President Jacob Zuma during the party's fifty-second conference, which was held in Polokwane, South Africa. (Alexander Joe/ AFP/Getty Images.)

use of all the means at our disposal, as the leading party in government, to achieve this. This objective should be reflected in the orientation and programmes of development finance institutions and regulatory bodies; through government procurement policies; in the sequencing of industrial and trade policy reforms; and in our macroeconomic policy stance.

We must work to further absorb the unemployed by promoting labour-intensive production methods and procurement policies, a significant expansion of public works programmes (linked to the massive expansion of economic infrastructure and meeting social needs), and an enlarged national youth service. . . .

Among the challenges that we . . . face is to respond effectively to the massive income inequality that continues to bedevil our society as we continue to make progress in pushing back the frontiers of poverty.

Our responses to poverty must seek to empower people to access economic opportunities, while creating a comprehensive social safety net to protect the most vulnerable in our society. We will accelerate the process of introduction of a mandatory retirement scheme.

> "Our teachers must commit to a set of non-negotiables—to be in school, in class, on time, teaching, no abuse of learners and no neglect of duty."

Education and health must be prioritised as the core elements of social transformation.

During the course of this year, we need to further enhance our efforts to improve the conditions of children and youth in poverty. We will need to attend to a number of Conference resolutions, including the proposal to gradually extend child support grants to 18 years, the development of a comprehensive strategy on early childhood development, and the progressive expansion of the school nutrition programme to include high school learners in poorer communities. . . .

Education and Public Health Must Be Supported

Over the next five years we need to undertake a concerted ANC-led campaign to support and promote the continued transformation of education.

This is a task that necessarily requires a longer view. Education must be elevated from being a departmental issue, or even a government issue, to a societal issue— one that occupies the attention and energy of all our people. . . .

Teachers are the critical element in our important task of ensuring quality education for all children. When our people faced the oppressive impact of Bantu Education [the racially discriminatory system under apartheid that severely restricted education for blacks], it was teachers who stood up and ensured that we confounded the architects of apartheid by producing doctors, lawyers and engineers. Now that we are free, we need a similar resolute commitment. Our teachers must commit to a set of non-negotiables—to be in school, in class, on time, teaching, no abuse of learners and no neglect of duty.

Similarly, we commit to restore, uphold and promote the status of teachers by remunerating them as professionals and improving the conditions in which they work. . . .

We must acknowledge that much is wrong in our public health care system. Though progress has been made, the country is still faced with significant challenges with respect to the quality of care provided; the physical infrastructure, maintenance and management of public health facilities; the working conditions and remuneration of doctors, nurses and other health care workers; and the inequitable distribution of health care resources.

CHAPTER **3**

Personal Narratives

Winning Freedom from the White Leadership

Nelson Mandela

In this excerpt from his autobiography, the man most central to the ending of apartheid—African National Congress (ANC) leader Nelson Mandela—tells how he negotiated freedom from imprisonment for himself and other ANC leaders with the last two presidents of the white minority government, P.W. Botha and F.W. de Klerk. The excerpt begins in 1986 with the black leader in solitary confinement and concludes with his 1990 release from prison.

In 1994, in the first all-races national election, Nelson Mandela was elected president of South Africa. He shared the 1993 Nobel Peace Prize with his predecessor, President F.W. de Klerk.

Photo on previous page: In Cape Town, outside South Africa's Houses of Parliament, the Presidential Guard marches prior to the bodies' 1996 opening ceremony. (**AP Images.**)

My solitude gave me a certain liberty, and I resolved to use it to do something I had been pondering for a long while: begin discussions with the government. I had concluded that the time had come when the struggle could best be pushed forward through negotiations. If we did not start a dialogue soon, both sides would be plunged into a dark night of oppression, violence, and war. My solitude would give me an opportunity to take the first steps in that direction, without the kind of scrutiny that might destroy such efforts.

We had been fighting against white minority rule for three-quarters of a century. We had been engaged in the armed struggle for more than two decades. Many people on both sides had already died. The enemy was strong and resolute. Yet even with all their bombers and tanks, they must have sensed they were on the wrong side of history. We had right on our side, but not yet might. It was clear to me that a militant victory was a distant if not impossible dream. It simply did not make sense for both sides to lose thousands if not millions of lives in a conflict that was unnecessary. They must have known this as well. It was time to talk.

This would be extremely sensitive. Both sides regarded discussions as a sign of weakness and betrayal. Neither would come to the table until the other made significant concessions. The government asserted over and over that we were a terrorist organization of Communists, and that they would never talk to terrorists or Communists. This was National Party dogma. The ANC [African National Congress] asserted over and over that the government was fascistic and racist and that there was nothing to talk about until they unbanned the ANC, unconditionally released all political prisoners, and removed the troops from the townships. . . .

> The first issue to arise [in negotiations with the government] was in many ways the most crucial, and that was the armed struggle.

[My] isolation furnished my organization with an excuse in case matters went awry: the old man was alone and completely cut off, and his actions were taken by him as an individual, not a representative of the ANC. . . .

Following his release from Victor Prison February 11, 1990, Nelson Mandela walks hand-in-hand with his wife, Winnie. (AP Images.)

Senior Officials Meet with Mandela

[After two years of preliminaries] the first formal meeting of the secret working group [of the government] took place in May 1988, at a posh officers' club within the precincts of Pollsmoor [prison]. While I knew both [Kobie] Coetsee and [Lieutenant General W.H.] Willemse, I had never before met [Fanie] van der Merwe and Dr. [Neil] Barnard. Van der Merwe was a quiet, levelheaded man who spoke only when he had something important to say. Dr. Barnard was in his mid-thirties and was exceedingly bright, a man of controlled intelligence and self-discipline.

The initial meeting was quite stiff, but in subsequent sessions we were able to talk more freely and directly. I met with them almost every week for a few months, and then the meetings occurred at irregular intervals, sometimes not for a month, and then suddenly every week. The meetings were usually scheduled by the government, but sometimes I would request a session.

During our early meetings, I discovered that my new colleagues, with the exception of Dr. Barnard, knew little about the ANC. They were all sophisticated Afrikaners, and far more open-minded than nearly all of their brethren. But they were the victims of so much propaganda that it was necessary to straighten them out about certain facts. Even Dr. Barnard, who had made a study of the ANC, had received most of his information from police and intelligence files, which were in the main inaccurate and sullied by the prejudices of the men who had gathered them. He could not help but be infected by the same biases.

I spent some time in the beginning sketching out the history of the ANC and then explaining our positions on the primary issues that divided the organization from the government. After these preliminaries, we focused on the critical issues: the armed struggle, the ANC's alliance with the Communist Party [CP], the goal of majority rule, and the idea of racial reconciliation.

The first issue to arise was in many ways the most crucial, and that was the armed struggle. We spent a number of months discussing it. They insisted that the ANC must renounce violence and give up the armed struggle before the government would agree to negotiations—and before I could meet President [P.W.] Botha. Their contention was that violence was nothing more than criminal behavior that could not be tolerated by the state.

I responded that the state was responsible for the violence and that it is always the oppressor, not the oppressed, who dictates the form of the struggle. If the oppressor uses violence, the oppressed have no alternative but to respond violently. In our case it was simply a legitimate form of self-defense. I ventured that if the state decided to use peaceful methods, the ANC would also use peaceful means. "It is up to you," I said, "not us, to renounce violence."

I think I advanced their understanding on this point, but the issue soon moved from a philosophical question to a practical one. As Minister Coetsee and Dr. Barnard pointed out, the National Party had repeatedly stated that it would not negotiate with any organization that advocated violence: therefore, how could it suddenly announce talks with the ANC without losing its credibility? In order for us to begin talks, they said, the ANC must make some compromise so that the government would not lose face with its own people.

It was a fair point and one that I could well understand, but I would not offer them a way out. "Gentlemen," I said, "it is not my job to resolve your dilemma for you." I simply told them that they must tell their people that there can be no peace and no solution to the situation in South Africa without sitting down with the ANC. People will understand, I said.

The Afrikaners Were Still Stuck in the Cold War

The ANC's alliance with the Communist Party seemed to trouble them almost as much as the armed struggle. The National Party accepted the most hidebound of 1950s cold war ideology and regarded the Soviet Union as the evil empire and communism as the work of the devil. There was nothing that one could do to disabuse them of this notion. They maintained that the Communist Party dominated and controlled the ANC and that in order for negotiations to begin we must break with the party.

First of all, I said, no self-respecting freedom fighter would take orders from the government he is fighting against or jettison a longtime ally in the interest of pleasing an antagonist. I then explained at great length that the party and the ANC were separate and distinct organizations that shared the same short-term objectives, the overthrow of racial oppression and the birth of a nonracial South Africa, but that our long-term interests were not the same.

> I told them that whites were Africans as well. . . . We do not want to drive you into the sea, I said.

This discussion went on for months. Like most Afrikaners, they thought that because many of the Communists in the ANC were white or Indian, they were controlling the blacks in the ANC. I cited many occasions when the ANC and the CP had differed on policy and the ANC had prevailed, but this did not seem to impress them. Finally, in exasperation, I said to them, "You gentlemen consider yourselves intelligent, do you not? You consider yourselves forceful and persuasive, do you not? Well, there are four of you and only one of me, and you cannot control me or get me to change my mind. What makes you think the Communists can succeed where you have failed?" . . .

Will White People Be Protected as a Minority?

The other main area of discussion was the issue of majority rule. They felt that if there was majority rule, the rights of minorities would be trampled. How would the ANC protect the rights of the white minority? they wanted to know. I said that there was no organization in the history of South Africa to compare with the ANC in terms of trying to unite all the people and races of South

Africa. I referred them to the preamble of the Freedom Charter: "South Africa belongs to all who live in it, black and white." I told them that whites were Africans as well, and that in any future dispensation the majority would need the minority. We do not want to drive you into the sea, I said.

The meetings had a positive effect: I was told in the winter of 1988 that President Botha was planning to see me before the end of August. The country was still in turmoil. The government had reimposed a State of Emergency in both 1987 and 1988. International pressure mounted. More companies left South Africa. The American Congress had passed a sweeping sanctions bill. . . .

At Last, Mandela Is to Meet with the President

On July 4 [1989], I was visited by General Willemse, who informed me that I was being taken to see President Botha the following day. He described the visit as a "courtesy call," and I was told to be ready to leave at 5:30 A.M. I told the general that while I was looking forward to the meeting, I thought it appropriate that I have a suit and tie in which to see Mr. Botha. . . . The general agreed, and a short while later, a tailor appeared to take my measurements. That afternoon I was delivered a new suit, tie, shirt, and shoes. Before leaving, the general also asked me my blood type, just in case anything untoward should happen the following day.

I prepared as best I could for the meeting. I reviewed my memo and the extensive notes I had made for it. I looked at as many newspapers and publications as I could to make sure I was up to date. After President Botha's resignation as head of the National Party, F.W. de Klerk had

> "The Great Crocodile [President P.W. Botha] . . . seemed to me to be the very model of the old-fashioned, stiff-necked, stubborn Afrikaner."

been elected in his place, and there was said to be considerable jockeying between the two men. Some might interpret Botha's willingness to meet me as his way of stealing thunder from his rival, but that did not concern me. I rehearsed the arguments that the state president might make and the ones I would put in return. In every meeting with an adversary, one must make sure one has conveyed precisely the impression one intends to.

I was tense about seeing Mr. Botha. He was known as *die Groot Krokodil*—the Great Crocodile—and I had heard many accounts of his ferocious temper. He seemed to me to be the very model of the old-fashioned, stiff-necked, stubborn Afrikaner who did not so much discuss matters with black leaders as dictate to them. His recent stroke had apparently only exacerbated this tendency. I resolved that if he acted in that finger-wagging fashion with me I would have to inform him that I found such behavior unacceptable, and I would then stand up and adjourn the meeting. . . .

From the opposite side of his grand office, P.W. Botha walked toward me. He had planned his march perfectly, for we met exactly halfway. He had his hand out and was smiling broadly, and in fact, from that very first moment, he completely disarmed me. He was unfailingly courteous, deferential, and friendly.

We very quickly posed for a photograph of the two of us shaking hands, and then were joined at a long table by Kobie Coetsee, General Willemse, and Dr. Barnard. Tea was served and we began to talk. From the first, it was not as though we were engaged in tense political arguments but a lively and interesting tutorial. We did not discuss substantive issues, so much as history and South African culture. I mentioned that I had recently read an article in an Afrikaans magazine about the 1914 Afrikaner Rebellion, and I mentioned how they had occupied towns in the Free State. I said I saw our struggle as parallel to this famous rebellion, and we discussed this historical episode for quite awhile. South African history, of course, looks very different to the black man than to the white man. Their view was that the rebellion had been a quarrel between brothers, whereas my struggle was a revolutionary one. I said that it could also be seen as a struggle between brothers who happen to be different colors.

Mandela Asks for Prisoners' Release

The meeting was not even half an hour, and was friendly and breezy until the end. It was then that I raised a serious issue. I asked Mr. Botha to release unconditionally all political prisoners, including myself. That was the only tense moment in the meeting, and Mr. Botha said that he was afraid that he could not do that.

There was then a brief discussion as to what we should say if news of the meeting leaked out. We very quickly drafted a bland statement saying that we had met for tea in an effort to promote peace in the country. When this was agreed upon, Mr. Botha rose and shook my hand, saying what a pleasure it had been. Indeed, it had been. I thanked him, and left the way we had come.

While the meeting was not a breakthrough in terms of negotiations, it was one in another sense. Mr. Botha had long talked about the need to cross the Rubicon, but he never did it himself until that morning at Tuynhuys [the president's office]. Now, I felt, there was no turning back.

A little more than a month later, in August 1989, P.W. Botha went on national television to announce his resignation as state president. In a curiously rambling farewell address, he accused cabinet members of a breach of trust, of ignoring him and of playing into the hands of the African National Congress. The following day, F.W. de Klerk was sworn in as acting president and affirmed his commitment to change and reform.

To us, Mr. de Klerk was a cipher. When he became head of the National Party, he seemed to be the quintessential party man, nothing more and nothing less. Nothing in his past seemed to hint at a spirit of reform. As education minister, he had attempted to keep black students out of white universities. But as soon as he took over the National Party, I began to follow him closely. I read all of his speeches, listened to what he said, and began to see that he represented a genuine departure from his predecessor. He was not an ideologue, but a pragmatist, a man who saw change as necessary and inevitable. On the day he was sworn in, I wrote him a letter requesting a meeting.

> [F.W.] De Klerk had lived up to his promise, and the [imprisoned] men were released under no bans; they could speak in the name of the ANC.

In his inaugural address, Mr. de Klerk said his government was committed to peace and that it would negotiate with any other group committed to peace. But his commitment to a new order was demonstrated only after his inauguration when a march was planned in Cape Town to protest police brutality. It was to be led by Archbishop [Desmond] Tutu and Reverend Allan Boesak. Under President Botha, the march would have been banned, marchers would have defied that ban, and violence would have resulted. The new president lived up to his promise to ease restrictions on political gatherings and permitted the march to take place, only asking that the demonstrators remain peaceful. A new and different hand was on the tiller.

Eight Political Prisoners Go Free

Even as de Klerk became president, I continued to meet with the secret negotiating committee. We were joined by Gerrit Viljoen, the minister of constitutional development, a brilliant man with a doctorate in classics, whose role was to bring our discussions into a constitutional framework. I pressed the government to display evidence of its good intentions, urging the state to show its bona fides by releasing my fellow political prisoners at Pollsmoor and Robben Island. While I told the committee that my colleagues had to be released unconditionally, I said the government could expect disciplined behavior from them after their release. That was demonstrated by the conduct of Govan Mbeki, who had been unconditionally released at the end of 1987.

On October 10, 1989, President de Klerk announced that Walter Sisulu and seven of my former Robben Island comrades, Raymond Mhlaba, Ahmed Kathrada, Andrew Mlangeni, Elias Motsoaledi, Jeff Masemola, Wilton Mkwayi, and Oscar Mpetha, were to be released. That morning, I had been visited by Walter, Kathy, Ray, and Andrew, who were still at Pollsmoor, and I was able to say good-bye. It was an emotional moment, but I knew I would not be too far behind. The men were released five days later from Johannesburg Prison. It was an action that rightly evoked praise here and abroad, and I conveyed my appreciation to Mr. de Klerk.

But my gratitude paled compared to my unalloyed joy that Walter and the others were free. It was a day we had yearned for and fought for over so many years. De Klerk had lived up to his promise, and the men were released under no bans; they could speak in the name of the ANC. It was clear that the ban on the organization had effectively expired, a vindication of our long struggle and our resolute adherence to principle.

> From the first I noticed that Mr. de Klerk listened to what I had to say. This was a novel experience.

De Klerk began a systematic dismantling of many of the building blocks of apartheid. He opened South African beaches to people of all colors, and stated that the Reservation of Separate Amenities Act would soon be repealed. Since 1953 this act had enforced what was known as "petty apartheid," segregating parks, theaters, restaurants, buses, libraries, toilets, and other public facilities, according to race. In November, he announced that the National Security Management System, a secret structure set up under P.W. Botha to combat anti-apartheid forces, would be dissolved.

In early December, I was informed that a meeting with de Klerk was set for the twelfth of that month. . . .

With guidance from a number of colleagues, I then drafted a letter to de Klerk not unlike the one I had sent to P.W. Botha. The subject was talks between the government and the ANC. I told the president that the current conflict was draining South Africa's lifeblood and talks were the only solution. I said the ANC would accept no preconditions to talks, especially not the precondition that the government wanted: the suspension of the armed struggle. The government asked for an "honest commitment to peace" and I pointed out that our readiness to negotiate was exactly that. . . .

On the morning of December 13, I was again taken to Tuynhuys. I met de Klerk in the same room where I had had tea with his predecessor. Mr. de Klerk was accompanied by Kobie Coetsee, General Willemse, Dr. Barnard, and his colleague Mike Louw. I congratulated Mr. de Klerk on becoming president and expressed the hope that we would be able to work together. He was extremely cordial and reciprocated these sentiments.

> In one sweeping action [de Klerk] had virtually normalized the situation in South Africa.

From the first I noticed that Mr. de Klerk listened to what I had to say. This was a novel experience. National Party leaders generally heard what they wanted to hear in discussions with black leaders, but Mr. de Klerk seemed to be making an attempt to truly understand. . . .

On February 2, 1990, F.W. de Klerk stood before Parliament to make the traditional opening speech and did something no other South African head of state had ever done: he truly began to dismantle the apartheid system and lay the groundwork for a democratic South Africa. In dramatic fashion, Mr. de Klerk announced the lifting of the bans on the ANC, the PAC, the South African Communist Party, and thirty-one other illegal organizations; the freeing of political prisoners incarcerated for nonviolent activities; the suspension of capital punishment; and the lifting of various restrictions imposed by the State of Emergency. "The time for negotiation has arrived," he said.

It was a breathtaking moment, for in one sweeping action he had virtually normalized the situation in South Africa. Our world had changed overnight. After forty years of persecution and banishment, the ANC was now a legal organization. I and all my comrades could no longer be arrested for being a member of the ANC, for carrying its green, yellow, and black banner, for speaking its name. For the first time in almost thirty years, my picture and my words, and those of all my banned comrades, could freely appear in South African newspapers. The international community applauded de Klerk's bold actions. Amidst all the good news, however, the ANC objected to the fact that Mr. de Klerk had not completely lifted the State of Emergency or ordered the troops out of the townships.

On February 9, seven days after Mr. de Klerk's speech opening Parliament, I was informed that I was again going to Tuynhuys. I arrived at six o'clock in the evening. I met a smiling Mr. de Klerk in his office and as we shook hands, he informed me that he was going to release me from prison the following day. Although the press in South Africa and around the world had been speculating for weeks that my release was imminent, Mr. de Klerk's announcement nevertheless came as a surprise to me. I had not been told that the reason Mr. de Klerk wanted to see me was to tell me that he was making me a free man.

A Teenage Afrikaner Begins to Break with His Powerful Family

Rian Malan

Afrikaners—white people of primarily Dutch ancestry—struggled for power with black Africans as well as British settlers over the centuries in South Africa. By 1948, though, Afrikaners ruled the country and imposed the white supremacist policy of apartheid. Rian Malan's family was instrumental in that history and in the ruling class. Born into the peak of apartheid, Malan, even as a child, rebelled against its unfairness, as he relates in this excerpt from his memoir.

In addition to his memoir, Rian Malan has written for *Time*, *Rolling Stone*, *The Observer*, *Esquire* and other publications. He has also written songs and made videos. He lives in Cape Town, South Africa.

SOURCE. Rian Malan, *My Traitor's Heart: A South African Exile Returns to Face His Country, His Tribe, and His Conscience*. London, UK: The Bodley Head, 1990. Copyright © 1990 Rian Malan. Reproduced by permission of Random House Group Limited.

I'm burned out and starving to death, so I'm just going to lay this all upon you and trust that you're a visionary reader, because the grand design, such as it is, is going to be hard for you to see. I know you're interested in my ancestors, so I guess I should begin at the very beginning. I am a Malan, descendant of Jacques Malan, a Huguenot who fled the France of Louis XIV to escape being put to the sword for his Protestant faith. He sought refuge among the Dutch, only to be put aboard ship in 1688 and sent to the Dark Continent, to the rude Dutch colony at the Cape of Good Hope. Jacques the Huguenot was the first Malan in Africa. In the centuries since, a Malan has been present at all the great dramas and turning points in the history of the Afrikaner tribe. . . .

What would you have me say? That I think apartheid is stupid and vicious? I do. That I'm sorry? I am, I am. That I'm not like the rest of them? If you'd met me a few years ago, in a bar in London or New York, I would have told you that. I would have told you that only I, of all my blind clan and tribe, had eyes that could truly see, and that what I saw appalled me. I would have passed myself off as a political exile, an enlightened sort who took black women into his bed and fled his country rather than carry a gun for the abominable doctrine of white supremacy. You would probably have believed me. I almost believed myself, you see, but in truth I was always one of them. I am a white man born in Africa, and all else flows from there. . . .

Unquestioning Childhood

In my childhood, there were always Africans in our backyard. We called them natives. They lived in cold, dark rooms with tiny windows. They put their beds on stacks of bricks, so that the mattresses stood waist-high to a grown man. This was to thwart a

> You wouldn't have known there were a million natives living [in the black township of Soweto], in regimented ranks of boxlike cement houses.

ground-hugging, night-prowling gremlin called the *toko-loshe*. The natives' quarters smelled of Lifebuoy soap, red floor polish, and *putu*, the stiff corn porridge that is the staple food of Africa. Natives cooked my meals, polished my shoes, made my bed, mowed the lawn, trimmed the hedge, and dug holes at my father's direction. They ate on enamel plates and drank out of chipped cups with no handles, which were known as the boy's cup or girl's cup and kept separate from the rest of our china. They spoke broken English or Afrikaans, wore old clothes, had no money and no last names. That was all it was really necessary to know about them.

On Thursdays, their day off, many natives donned Crusader robes of blue or green and tied white sashes across their chests. They took up their staves and shepherd's crooks and set forth for the nearest stretch of undeveloped land, where they sang and danced in circles around fires. There was a place near our home called the Dip, a steep valley that separated the suburbs of Victory Park and Parkhurst. Looking down into the Dip on Thursday afternoons, you saw at least a dozen columns of smoke and a dozen rings of dancing Zionists. The drums of Africa were beating in the humdrum heart of white suburbia, but that sound made virtually no impression on me as a child. I never asked Zionists who they were worshiping, and why. I never made a point of finding out what the *tokoloshe* looked like and whether he might get me, too. Natives put their beds on bricks, Zionists danced on Thursdays, and thunderstorms washed streaks of red African earth into the streets. These were signs of Africa, but almost all of us were blind to them.

> Loving natives was a very good investment.

Some natives lived in white backyards, and some lived elsewhere—over those hills, beyond the mine dumps, beyond the industrial wastelands, in a desolate and despairing place called Soweto. On winter evenings, the acrid smoke of cooking fires came drifting over the horizon from that direction. Otherwise, you wouldn't have known there were a million natives living there, in regimented ranks of boxlike cement houses that marched over the horizon in all directions. . . .

Insistent Love

Maybe it was the love of a prince for his loyal subjects, and conditional upon their remaining loyal and subservient, but I loved natives anyway. The first one I loved was Johannes, our garden boy before I went to school. Johannes looked after me while my mother was away teaching. I followed him everywhere. When he was tired, I made him come inside and sit in my father's armchair. I made him put his feet up and served him tea. Ah, yes—a revealing choice of word. I was only five years old, but already I was giving orders. I *made* Johannes accept my gestures of love. Was I any more to him than a bossy white child? I don't know, because he went away, or we went away, and James eventually came in his place. James taught me to play Zulu walking guitar, and then he went away, too, and along came Piet.

Piet was a squat, ugly Tswana. He drank and smoked *zol*—dope—but he had spirit, and big dreams. He once bought some rabbits and made a pen for them on the compost heap behind the shed. He was going to breed and butcher them to make some money. It was a secret from my father, but he let me in on it. One day our dog got into the pen, and that was the end of the rabbits. Another time, Piet bought one of those motor tricycles with a box on the back, the kind delivery boys drove. He was going to fix it up and make a business taking things home to Pietersburg for other natives, but he never could get it going. Piet and I spent hours lying shoulder to shoulder in the dirt between the peach trees in my father's garden, shooting rats in the hedge with my pellet gun. He bought beer for me when I was too young to be drinking legally,

> "My father supported apartheid. . . . In his eyes, it was a sensible solution to the problems of a multiethnic society."

and scored the first *zol* I ever smoked. When Phillip Nel and his gang were sitting on my chest, beating me, it was Piet Maribatse who pulled them off. Piet was my good friend. Hey, what can I say; I loved him.

I loved them all, indiscriminately: Lena, Johannes, Piet, James, Betty, Miriam, Miriam's children and teeming grandchildren, the other Piet, who worked next door, the waiters in the hotel down the road, John's boys—all of them. Loving natives was a very good investment. I learned that at the very beginning, and it remains true to this day. If you were friendly, they lit up and laughed and returned your love a hundredfold. It seemed so easy and ordinary to love them then. Maybe we are all that way in the beginning. Maybe we just grow out of it, or are taught otherwise. When I was a little older, I began to notice that many whites around me felt otherwise about blacks. . . .

A Bold Letter

When I was in the ninth or tenth grade, an Indian revolutionary named Ahmed Timol "fell" to his death from a tenth-floor window while undergoing interrogation by the secret police. Ahmed Timol was the twelfth man on the list of detainees who'd died suspiciously in the custody of the secret police, falling somewhere between the Islamic imam who "fell down a flight of stairs" and Steve Biko, who "struck his head on a bench" during a "fight" with his interrogators. Something sinister was obviously afoot, so I wrote a letter to *The Star*, Johannesburg's dominant daily, expressing my Afrikaner's dismay over the manner in which Timol died, and my Afrikaner's insistence on a thorough and impartial inquiry.

In those days, an Afrikaner with a conscience was still something of a novelty, even if he was only fourteen. A day or two later, my letter appeared at the head of the letters-to-the-editor page, under a huge headline reading, "An Afrikaner Speaks Out." At the bottom, in bold type, it said "—Rian Malan, Linden."

It was a day of delirious triumph for me largely because my childish scribblings had been accorded such adult weight and dignity. Mrs. Pretorius, the neighbor, rang up to congratulate me. Two schoolteachers called to commend me. My Uncle John called from Parys, chuckling, "Ho, ho, ho, what's all this, then?"

Toward evening, my father came home, poured himself a whiskey, and sat down to read the afternoon papers. My father supported apartheid, moderately, and didn't mind moderate criticisms of it. In his eyes, it was a sensible solution to the problems of a multiethnic society—the only solution. It wasn't perfect, but you couldn't change things overnight. He truly believed apartheid's central lie, its promise to create a world in which blacks and whites were separate but equal, and he was incapable of seeing the suffering it was inflicting meanwhile. In some ways, he was a wise and compassionate man—wise enough, several years later, to talk a friend of mine down from a bad acid trip. In other ways, he was completely blind. It seemed very strange to me.

He paged through *The Star*'s news and business sections, scanning the headlines, and came at last to the letters page. He read my letter and let the paper fall to his lap. He took off his glasses and gave me a dirty look, I thought he was about to offer his standard argument, which ran thus: The secret police know more than you do. If they lock somebody up, there must be a reason for it; and if they say Timol fell, he surely fell. But he didn't say that. He just said, "What gives you the right to call yourself an Afrikaner?" Then he lifted the paper and turned to the sports page.

A Young Activist Overcomes Fear and Emptiness, but Dies in the Struggle

Steve Biko

In this 1970 excerpt from a book of his writings, Steve Biko defines black consciousness in the context of apartheid. He urges black Africans to stand up for themselves, to celebrate the virtues of their culture and their humanity, and to cast aside spiritual poverty.

A medical student who became a political activist, Steve Biko became so influential he was a particular target of the apartheid police apparatus. The final time he was jailed, in 1977, he was killed while in custody.

SOURCE. Steve Biko, *I Write What I Like*. New York: Harper & Row, 1978. Copyright © 1978 The Bowerdean Press. Previously unpublished writings of Steve Biko copyright © 1978 by N.M. Biko. Reproduced by permission of HarperCollins Publishers Inc.

Born shortly before 1948, I have lived all my conscious life in the framework of institutionalised separate development. My friendships, my love, my education, my thinking and every other facet of my life have been carved and shaped within the context of separate development. In stages during my life I have managed to outgrow some of the things the system taught me. Hopefully what I propose to do now is to take a look at those who participate in opposition to the system—not from a detached point of view but from the point of view of a black man, conscious of the urgent need for an understanding of what is involved in the new approach—"black consciousness".

One needs to understand the basics before setting up a remedy. A number of the organisations now currently "fighting against apartheid" are working on an oversimplified premise. They have taken a brief look at what is, and have diagnosed the problem incorrectly. They have almost completely forgotten about the side effects and have not even considered the root cause. Hence whatever is improvised as a remedy will hardly cure the condition.

Apartheid—both petty and grand—is obviously evil. Nothing can justify the arrogant assumption that a clique of foreigners has the right to decide on the lives of a majority. Hence even carried out faithfully and fairly the policy of apartheid would merit condemnation and vigorous opposition from the indigenous peoples as well as those who see the problem in its correct perspective. The fact that apartheid has been tied up with white supremacy, capitalist exploitation, and deliberate oppression makes the problem much more complex. Material want is bad enough, but coupled with spiritual poverty it kills. And this latter effect is probably the one that creates

> Reduced to an obliging shell, [the black man] looks with awe at the white power structure.

> A people without a positive history is like a vehicle without an engine.

mountains of obstacles in the normal course of emancipation of the black people. . . .

Black Men Have Been Dehumanized

To a large extent the evil-doers have succeeded in producing at the output end of their machine a kind of black man who is man only in form. This is the extent to which the process of dehumanisation has advanced.

Black people under the [Jan] Smuts government [prime minister of South Africa, 1919–24 and 1939–48] were oppressed but they were still men. They failed to change the system for many reasons which we shall not consider here. But the type of black man we have today has lost his manhood. Reduced to an obliging shell, he looks with awe at the white power structure and accepts what he regards as the "inevitable position". Deep inside his anger mounts at the accumulating insult, but he vents it in the wrong direction—on his fellow man in the township, on the property of black people. No longer does he trust leadership, for the 1963 mass arrests were blameable on bungling by the leadership, nor is there any to trust. In the privacy of his toilet his face twists in silent condemnation of white society but brightens up in sheepish obedience as he comes out hurrying in response to his master's impatient call. In the home-bound bus or train he joins the chorus that roundly condemns the white man but is first to praise the government in the presence of the police or his employers. His heart yearns for the comfort of white society and makes him blame himself for not having been "educated" enough to warrant such luxury. Celebrated achievements by whites in the field of science—which he understands only hazily—serve to make him rather convinced of the futility of resistance and to throw away any hopes that change may ever come.

All in all the black man has become a shell, a shadow of man, completely defeated, drowning in his own misery, a slave, an ox bearing the yoke of oppression with sheepish timidity.

This *is* the first truth, bitter as it may seem, that we have to acknowledge before we can start on any programme designed to change the status quo. It becomes more necessary to see the truth as it is if you realise that the only vehicle for change are these people who have lost their personality. The first step therefore is to make the black man come to himself; to pump back life into his empty shell; to infuse him with pride and dignity, to remind him of his complicity in the crime of allowing himself to be misused and therefore letting evil reign supreme in the country of his birth. This is what we mean by an inward-looking process. This is the definition of "Black Consciousness." . . .

Where Are the African Heroes?

No doubt . . . part of the approach envisaged in bringing about "black consciousness" has to be directed to the past, to seek to rewrite the history of the black man and to produce in it the heroes who form the core of the African background. To the extent that a vast literature about Gandhi in South Africa is accumulating it can be said that the Indian community already has started in this direction. But only scant reference is made to African heroes. A people without a positive history is like a vehicle without an engine. Their emotions cannot be easily controlled and channelled in a recognisable direction. They always live in the shadow of a more successful society. Hence in a country like ours they are forced to celebrate holidays like Paul Kruger's day, Heroes' day, Republic day etc.—all of which are occasions during which the humiliation of defeat is at once revived.

Then too one can extract from our indigenous cultures a lot of positive virtues which should teach the

Westerner a lesson or two. The oneness of community for instance is at the heart of our culture. The easiness with which Africans communicate with each other is not forced by authority but is inherent in the make-up of African people. Thus whereas the white family can stay in an area without knowing its neighbours, Africans develop a sense of belonging to the community within a short time of coming together. Many a hospital official has been confounded by the practice of Indians who bring gifts and presents to patients whose names they can hardly recall. Again this is a manifestation of the interrelationship between man and man in the black world as opposed to the highly impersonal world in which Whitey lives. These are characteristics we must not allow ourselves to lose.

> The bible must . . . preach that it is a sin to allow oneself to be oppressed.

Their value can only be appreciated by those of us who have not as yet been made slaves to technology and the machine. One can quote a myriad of other examples. Here again "black consciousness" seeks to show the black people the value of their own standards and outlook. It urges black people to judge themselves according to these standards and not to be fooled by white society who have white-washed themselves and made white standards the yardstick by which even black people judge each other. . . .

Christianity Shows Up in Different Colors

What of the white man's religion—Christianity? It seems the people involved in imparting Christianity to the black people steadfastly refuse to get rid of the rotten foundation which many of the missionaries created when they came. To this date black people find no message for them in the Bible simply because our ministers are still too busy with moral trivialities. They blow these

Photo on next page: On September 13, 1987, the tenth anniversary of Steven Biko's death, a poster depicting the slain South African Black Consciousness leader rests amid flowers during commemoration ceremonies in Soweto. (AP Images.)

WE PAY TRIBUTE TO
STEVE

up as the most important things that Jesus had to say to people. They constantly urge the people to find fault in themselves and by so doing detract from the essence of the struggle in which the people are involved. Deprived of spiritual content, the black people read the bible with a gullibility that is shocking. While they sing in a chorus of "mea culpa" they are joined by white groups who sing a different version—"tua culpa". The anachronism of a well-meaning God who allows people to suffer continually under an obviously immoral system is not lost to young blacks who continue to drop out of Church by the hundreds. Too many people are involved in religion for the blacks to ignore. Obviously the only path open for us now is to redefine the message in the bible and to make it relevant to the struggling masses. The bible must not be seen to preach that all authority is divinely instituted. It must rather preach that it is a sin to allow oneself to be oppressed. The bible must continually be shown to have something to say to the black man to keep him going in his long journey towards realization of the self. This is the message implicit in "black theology". Black theology seeks to do away with spiritual poverty of the black people. It seeks to demonstrate the absurdity of the assumption by whites that "ancestor worship" was necessarily a superstition and that Christianity is a scientific religion. While basing itself on the Christian message, black theology seeks to show that Christianity is an adaptable religion that fits in with the cultural situation of the people to whom it is imparted. Black theology seeks to depict Jesus as a fighting God who saw the exchange of Roman money—the oppressor's coinage—in His father's temple as so sacrilegious that it merited a violent reaction from Him—the Son of Man.

Thus in all fields "Black Consciousness" seeks to talk to the black man in a language that is his own. It is only by recognising the basic set-up in the black world that one will come to realise the urgent need for a re-awakening of the sleeping masses. Black consciousness seeks to do this. Needless to say it shall have to be the black people themselves who shall take care of this programme.

In Ending Apartheid, the White Government Delivers on Its Promises

F.W. de Klerk

In the following selection from the autobiography of the last white president of apartheid South Africa, F.W. de Klerk looks back on his leadership. For the most part, he says, he succeeded, especially in ending apartheid peacefully. He acknowledges that mistakes were made and many problems persist, but he notes that all South Africans have made significant progress by achieving a free and democratic society.

F.W. de Klerk's presidency lasted from 1989 until he lost the election to Nelson Mandela in 1994. He and Mandela shared the 1993 Nobel Peace Prize.

One of the most common questions I nowadays have to deal with is: what would you have done differently, if you were given the opportunity?

SOURCE. F.W. de Klerk, *The Last Trek—A New Beginning*. New York: St. Martin's Press, 1998. Copyright © 1998 F.W. de Klerk. Reproduced by permission.

And by many white South Africans I am asked whether, in the final analysis, I took the right course on 2 February 1990.

> Those who criticize the result of negotiation now, forget how hopeless our situation seemed in 1988.

I have reflected deeply on this. Such questions confront everyone at the end of a career or a specific phase in their lives—questions which require deep self-analysis and honesty. Without such honesty, the result is usually self-serving rationalization. In the full awareness of this pitfall, I nevertheless remain convinced that all the most important decisions that the National Party and I took since 1989 were necessary and in the best interest of all South Africans—including my own people. I would once again accept co-responsibility for the National Party's decision to make a total break with the policy of separate development and to accept a new vision. I would still have worked for a united South Africa with a single citizenship, a one-man-one-vote franchise, and the abolition of all forms of discrimination on the grounds of race or colour. I would still have tried to negotiate a constitution which would seek a balance between equal rights for all and a fair form of protection for cultural and religious minorities; which would contain a strong and justiciable Charter of Basic Human Rights; and which would find a reasonable balance between the proper powers of central and provincial governments. I would once again repeat my speech of 2 February 1990 and, in the end, would once again say yes to both the interim and final constitutions. I would do so despite the clear shortcomings which exist in both constitutions with regard to the full realization of the goals for which the National Party and I strove in the negotiations. I would once again call a referendum, again decide that the atom bombs that we possessed should be dismantled, again repeal all discriminatory legislation before the election of April 1994, again accept the result of the 1994 election despite the many irregularities, again lead the National Party out of the Government of National Unity and again decide to retire from active politics on the date on which I did.

Naturally, I must also admit to mistakes with regard to these and many other matters. In particular, I should have managed the negotiations on the TRC [Truth and Reconciliation Commission] process differently. In retrospect I should have insisted much more strongly on guarantees for an even-handed process, in which all the parties to the conflict of the past would have been equal owners of the process—even if that would have caused a crisis of major proportions. . . .

The Power-Sharing Aspect Fell Short

In retrospect, my greatest disappointment in the constitutional field relates to our lack of success in producing a power-sharing model suited to the needs of our complex nation. It is widely accepted that in deeply divided societies such as ours, it is essential that all the major components of society, should feel that they are meaningfully represented and included in the processes by which they are governed. The alternative is exactly the kind of alienation, division and mounting rage which now threatens our future success. The majoritarian reality which has now, to a certain extent, been thrust on us contains the clear threat of the kind of racial domination which must be avoided at all costs.

Those who criticize the result of negotiation now, forget how hopeless our situation seemed in 1988—or how perilous it was in the months before the election in 1994. Anyone who would have predicted then that we would be able to bring the IFP [Inkatha Freedom Party] and the Freedom Front into the elections; that we would be able to defuse the threat of right-wing violence; that we would be able to hold the elections with reasonable success; that the ANC-led government would adopt

F.W. de Klerk, former South African president and the reformer who negotiated apartheid's end, speaks at a press conference, discussing his resignation on August 26, 1997. (**AP Images.**)

responsible economic policies and that the country would be broadly at peace with itself four years after the transformation, would have been accused of hopeless optimism. The reality is that despite all our problems we are in a far better position now than we would have been had we failed to act as we did.

> We have become an inspiration for other divided societies throughout the world.

I maintain that we have substantially delivered on our referendum promises. Those who say that we did not are generally speaking people who either voted 'no' in the referendum and/or people who incorrectly expected that we would achieve a white minority veto. This we never advocated.

Simultaneously, those who are critical should also not underestimate the remarkable progress that we have all made during the past ten years, nor our historic achievement in creating the new South Africa. They should constantly remind themselves of the tremendous gains that the new South Africa has brought them—and the perils that they have avoided by resolving centuries of division and bitterness in a reasonably peaceful and sensible manner.

After three centuries of struggle black, coloured and Indian South Africans have at last been liberated from the restrictions, powerlessness and injustices of the past. That liberation has brought with it all the rights and privileges which they were, to a greater or lesser extent, denied for generations. And with those rights have come the corresponding responsibilities. They are now, together with all their fellow South Africans, in charge of their own destiny.

We have avoided the racial cataclysm that so many observers believed was unavoidable. We have proved that even the most intractable and complex problems can be resolved through compromise, negotiations and goodwill. By so doing we have become an inspiration for other divided societies throughout the world.

We have established a free and truly democratic society with a constitution and a charter of fundamental rights that can compare with the best in the world.

It is not only black, coloured and Indian South Africans who have been liberated. After generations, whites have been freed from the defensive *laager* [military camp defended by a formation of ox-wagons] in which they had for centuries been confined. . . .

We Now Have Security and Hope

And so we have at last arrived at our destination—the new South Africa. It is sometimes frightening, but always exciting and exhilarating. We no longer view our continent from behind defensive positions—of stone or ox-wagons or discriminatory laws. But we are not without protection. Our new constitution now gives all South Africans a reasonable degree of security. We can now confront the challenges of our country together with all our fellow South Africans. We can share common aspirations and work for common goals unencumbered by the baggage of discrimination—with no greater nor lesser rights than any of our fellow countrymen. I believe that we have at last come to terms with the realities of our continent. We have completed a great spiritual trek. We are ready for a new beginning.

Teens Open Up About Their Lives After Apartheid

Leandra Jansen van Vuuren, Nithinia Martin, and Nomfundo Mhlana

After apartheid ended and Nelson Mandela was elected president, author Tim McKee interviewed teenagers around South Africa. The following selection includes accounts from three teens: Leandra Jansen van Vuuren, a white South African, or Afrikaner; Nithinia Martin, who is mixed race, or coloured; and Nomfundo Mhlana, a black South African. Their experiences are vastly different, but all share a hope for a better future in postapartheid South Africa.

SOURCE. Leandra Jansen van Vuuren, Nithinia Martin, and Nomfundo Mhlana, *No More Strangers Now: Young Voices from a New South Africa.* New York: DK Publishing, 1998. Text copyright © 1998 by Timothy Saunders McKee. Used by permission of Penguin Group (USA) Inc.

Leandra Jansen van Vuuren

*M*ost white schools, churches, and communities supported apartheid's notion that black South Africans were inferior to whites. Now that South Africans are allowed to mix freely, many whites are beginning to realize how shallow and racist their perceptions of Africans were. But biases still run deep, especially in South Africa's small rural towns, where segregation and mistrust remain the norm.

Fifteen-year-old Leandra Jansen van Vuuren comes from one such town, Potgietersrus, tucked amid white farms in the northern part of the country. Potgietersrus was the subject of worldwide attention in 1996, when white parents blocked a public elementary school's entrance to keep black pupils from attending.

When I was small I was told I had to stay away from black people because they were almost like animals: They were dangerous, they could kill you. I used to overhear my aunt telling my mother that blacks were going to take over our houses, kill the women and children and that the men were not allowed to leave their children and wives at home. My father had a .22 rifle, and he said, "Okay, my darling, if they come into our house, we'll just kill them."

> **The thing that changed me most was going to a weekend camp with black kids and Indians.**

My father raises chickens and pigs on our farm, and I used to go with him when he'd sell them in the black townships. I'd see black kids there, but I'd just walk away from them. It was almost like, "No, you can stay there and I'll stay here. You must be away from me." I'd say things like, "Hey, look at the *kaffir!*" I thought it was just a way to describe a black person; I didn't know then that it wasn't nice. The white kids around me also grew up on farms, and they never mixed with blacks either.

To me it just seemed that blacks and whites were in different places. At school and church there were only whites; they didn't tell us about the way blacks lived. I didn't know what was happening to black people, that things were unfair. They taught us about all the dead Afrikaners that the blacks had killed, to be proud of the places where Afrikaners died for us, and that Afrikaners had done good things for South Africa.

So when I heard that apartheid was going away, I hated it. I thought, Why must they move near us, why must they take our land over, why must they mix with us? When I'd visit my nephew near Pretoria and we'd see black kids who had moved close, we'd chase them on bikes, and we'd yell, "Hey, why are you coming here?"

> I think you can teach your parents that it's not right to be racist against other people. My father will be glad after I explain it to him.

Even last year, when black kids first tried to come to our school, I saw white parents who stood outside the gates and tried to stop them from coming. I kind of agreed with them, like, why can't the blacks stay in their own schools? And when the blacks did come in, the white kids said, "They're a bunch of idiots; they can't even write." I said it as well.

I began to change a bit when our church began to have black people in it. I mean, if you love God, you love God. The Bible says that God inspired the people to rise in all nations. Everybody should be welcome in the church, and I saw that those churches that didn't want to let blacks in were not right.

The thing that changed me most was going to a weekend camp with black kids and Indians. When I first came to the camp, all the kids were eating, and they said, "Come, come, sit by us." I first felt a bit out with the black ones, and the first night I thought I had to be careful. But then we began to play cricket and soccer, and I saw that

Indians, whites, and blacks, all the colors, were playing together.

We also had to find a "buddy" who was different from us, and I found a black girl. Her hair felt a bit tough, not the same as ours, not fine. Her eyes were brown, and when she would talk, they'd go so big like she had a fright. She talked louder than me and had different traditions, but in other ways we were the same. She wore the same kind of clothes as me, long pants and a normal T-shirt. She was a Christian, too.

I will keep in touch with all the friends I made at camp. It's better to have a friend than to have no friend, even if that person looks different from me. My buddy lives in a township, and if she asks me over, I'll go. When I get together with her, we're going to play, of course. But I'd also like to learn some things from her culture, like dance. And I'd like to learn her language. People always like you more if you can speak their language.

It's strange that just by eating with someone or going to church with someone, you can begin to see them. Earlier this year before I went to camp, I saw shacks in the city where black people were living, and I laughed. But you know, now I'm learning more, and I see that if we had to live in that, we wouldn't laugh, we wouldn't think it was a joke. I used to think it was all right when I'd see stories on TV about how white policemen used to hit black people. But now I see they are also human beings, and they need a chance to live. After fourteen years of not mixing very much, just two days made me start to think differently.

At first I don't think my father is going to like to hear that I'm playing with blacks because he's not very used to it. But I think you can teach your parents that it's not right to be racist against other people. My father will be glad after I explain it to him because I will tell him that it's time to learn how to make friends, because if we don't have that, what are we going to do?

> Even though I had black relatives, I was always taught to curse my own blackness because it prevented me from being white.

Most of the kids at school don't know what I've learned. If a black girl comes close, a lot of them will just move away. I can see that they are afraid to mix; I know this because I was afraid, too. But I've made a new beginning, and I think it's important now to try and change things at my school. The message I want to give is that everyone must learn to respect one another and that will make life far easier. Apartheid gave us a very bad image of the blacks; it didn't tell us the truth. That is what we have to change, so that we see them as they really are, nor what we think they are. If we don't respect them, we won't ever have a day when we say, "We're sorry, we were blind."

Nithinia Martin

The Population Registration Act of 1950 classified all South Africans by race so that the government could ensure that each citizen was in his or her proper place on the apartheid ladder.

In the middle of this racial caste system were Coloureds [those of mixed race], who constitute 9 percent of South Africa's population. Like Africans, Coloureds were forced to live in townships, accept inferior education, and take only low-paying jobs. But Coloureds were also placed one rung above Africans, living in communities and attending schools with slightly better resources than their African counterparts.

Eighteen-year-old Nithinia Martin lives in Westbury, a Coloured township in Johannesburg located between the white suburb of Westdene and the African township of Soweto.

As a Coloured, apartheid taught me basically that I'm better than blacks but that I can never be white. We were on the fence, stuck in the middle.

Whites were sly. They gave Coloureds a bit higher position than blacks and told us that we're better than them. They must have feared that if we got to know blacks and saw the good in them, then we might interact and start becoming one, and that united, we might have destroyed the whole system. Like in the last elections, most Coloureds voted for Mandela, and see he won, because we stood together.

So I grew up thinking just like the apartheid government wanted me to. Even though I had black relatives, I was always taught to curse my own blackness because it prevented me from being white. I was angry about my parts that were black; I grew my hair long and used a hair relaxer to make it thin, so that I would not look like a black person. And I saw whites as superior. Whenever I had contact with them, they were dressed well and drove nice cars. When I saw the way whites were portrayed on TV, I thought, That's the ideal way of living. I'd always say to myself, If only my hair was straight and I had blue eyes, I'd be white. . . .

It was all really confusing to me. On the one hand, I admired whites, and on the other, I sort of hated them because I knew they were oppressing us. Apartheid made it so that whites who didn't even finish school could get proper jobs, while blacks and Coloureds who *had* finished school couldn't. I think that's why my father got involved in gangs. He didn't finish school, and he was Coloured, so it was almost impossible to find work. With gangs he could make a living.

When I was about three or four years old, my father got arrested for the murder of another gangster, even though people say he didn't do it. He was in jail for a few years, and then he got sentenced to death. I remember visiting him in prison and my grandmother telling me to say good-bye because I wouldn't see him again. My eyes were watering because I wanted to cry, but I just said good-bye. That's the only way I can remember my father, sitting behind a glass. I can remember seeing tears in his eyes, just looking at me, staring at me, saying nothing.

After my dad died, two of his brothers were also killed because of the gangs. I lived with his mother, my granny, because my parents were never married and I didn't know my mom then. My granny started selling drugs because when her sons died, there wasn't enough money for all of us to live on. Drug addicts would come to my granny and sell their gold watches, wedding bands, furniture, expensive things, just for a few pills. I'd sell to people when they'd come to the house. I saw how those drugs would destroy people, destroy families. But I sold anyway, because I thought I was helping my family and it was the right thing to do. When the police would come, my gran would give us kids the drugs to keep because the police wouldn't search us. I'd keep them in my hands or shove them in my socks. I'd be so scared.

> It's like we Coloureds aren't black enough now, just like we weren't white enough before.

Last year my granny finally decided she was causing too much pain and stopped selling drugs. Now gangs are the main salesman. Gangs have gotten worse here since my dad's days. Before, they fought only with stones and knives, but now everyone has guns. Westbury is so violent now; you don't know where to walk or when you might get killed. Whatever the gangsters do, nobody does nothing about it because people are too scared to say anything.

There are so many guys involved in drugs and gangs because there's no sense of hope in our community; it's very dim. In a way I feel we Coloureds are still stuck in the middle. Now it's almost like everything's just the opposite. Before it was white, now it's black, but it's like we Coloureds aren't black enough now, just like we weren't white enough before. We're getting passed over in things like affirmative action, even though we stood by blacks before. . . .

I just finished high school, and I hope to go to university and study psychology. But right now my granny can't afford to send me. When she stopped selling drugs, the struggle really began. Twelve of us live in one house, and we live off my aunt's small salary and my granny's pension. There are times when at the end of the month we have to borrow money to pay for food.

> I've learned to be proud to be a Coloured and to just be myself.

But I have faith that I can make it out of here somehow. I've been attending a multiracial church for four years, and it's really helped me appreciate who I am. Through meeting whites there, I've seen that they can also make mistakes and that it's no use looking up to them. They're just the same; it's only the color, the hair, and the eyes that are different. And by getting to know blacks, I've realized that being black is a blessing, not a curse. Now when I hear Coloureds being racist, I reprimand them: "Now why are you putting blacks down? You're just as black as they are!"

I've learned to be proud to be a Coloured and to just be myself. I feel comfortable and confident with who I am. I decided a few years ago that it's my choice, that I can be angry at the whole world for the situation I've grown up in and be as messed up as everyone else, or I can start living and planning my future. I have a rich heritage, with both black and white in me, and I feel I can be an important part of the South African picture.

Nomfundo Mhlana

The Land Act of 1913 is a prime example of the unequal distribution of land that has characterized South Africa's history. The act put aside 93 percent of the country's most arable land for white farmers and allowed Africans, who made up roughly 75 percent of the population, to own land only in the dry, overpopulated areas that remained. This forced many Africans to work on white farms, where they lived in small shacks beside the elaborate houses of their employers.

Nineteen-year-old Nomfundo Mhlana comes from a family that for several generations has worked for white farmers near Grootfontein in the Karoo, a vast expanse of flatland in the heart of South Africa.

> "When I saw the way our parents worked for the whites, I thought the whites were superior to us and that their white skin made them rich."

I grew up on a white person's farm, where my father worked with the sheep in the fields and my mother cleaned the white person's house. My parents never even got a whole day off; they worked all 365 days of the year.

When I was small, I saw the bad way the whites treated my parents. When the farmers went to work, for example, they wanted my mom to take care of their babies. My mother and the white babies began to love each other—when my mother was playing with the baby, the baby would laugh—but when the babies got older, their parents would tell them, "This is a black, and she is working for us. She is not like us." They didn't really see us as the same kind of human beings.

My mother was not friends with the white woman. I think the white lady liked my mom when she was working, but not other times. She gave her an Afrikaans name, Rosie, even though her real name is Nofozile. The whites knew that name, but they said they couldn't call her that because they couldn't say the name correctly.

As a child I felt bad about being black. When I saw the way our parents worked for the whites, I thought the whites were superior to us and that their white skin made them rich. I would look at the color of my skin and then look at the whites' color, and I would think, I wish I was white.

Growing up on that farm, I didn't go to school until I was ten years old. The whites discouraged my brother and me from going to school because they were worried that we would get some knowledge and then want change. If I went to school, maybe I'd never come back and work in the farm kitchen.

So when I was small, I was learning at home and playing. My brother and I played with the white kids, but not as equals. If we were playing hard and hitting each other. I couldn't hit the white. I could call the children by their names, except if they were bigger than me. Then I called them *klein baas* [little boss]. The white children had things I did not have; they had cars that worked with batteries and dolls that cried when you put them down.

> Now that Mandela is president, I think our society is more equal, but I also think whites still have apartheid in their hearts.

We lived far from where the whites lived because the whites didn't want the noise from the black workers. I always wanted to go inside the "big house" because I could see outside there were grasses and flowers, so I thought that the inside of the house would be very interesting. But I was never allowed to go into the house because the whites thought that if I came in there, my shoes would make the house dirty or I would steal something. The whites knew that the blacks didn't have the things that they had, so they didn't trust the black workers. They would always keep a list of their sheep, for example, because they thought their black workers would steal one.

I went inside the big house for the first time when I was fourteen years old, when I came to talk with my mother in the kitchen. I was afraid the whites would chase me out, but I went in anyway. When I saw videos and TV and the rugs on the ground, I was angry. I thought, Why doesn't my home look like this? How

> My education will give me an advantage; it will help me get better jobs.

could the whites have so many things and so many rooms in their house but my parents have nothing?

Now that Mandela is president, I think our society is more equal, but I also think whites still have apartheid in their hearts. They pay workers more because the democratic government says they must and because they're afraid of the law. But they still think they are better than us. We now live on a different farm than when I was a child, and my parents still have to call the whites *baas*. They still don't pay workers enough money. My parents have six children, and they would like to live in a nice house, but they only have enough money for food.

But I do have hope that some whites are changing their minds. The whites on the farm now will come into our house and drink some tea with my mother. They also have a daughter who is nineteen, like me, and we are friends. When she comes to ride horses, she greets me, and when I have something I don't know at school, I go to ask her, and she helps me. I'm now going to a school that was started by white farmers' wives, for children on the farms like me. The farmers at our place think it's okay that my brother and I are in this school, and they say that education is the best thing to have. In fact, they came to a party when the school first opened.

I will not work on the farm like my parents. They were illiterate and living in the times of apartheid, and working on the farm was all they could do. But my education will give me an advantage; it will help me get better jobs than they could. I want to have a career in social work because I love to talk to children and I don't like to see them being abused. I know that I won't make that much money as a social worker, but I hope that I will make enough to buy a house and let my family live there with me. Then they won't have to work on the farm anymore. My parents worked hard to allow me to go to school, and I must make them proud.

When I was small, I was jealous of whites; I wanted to be like them. But now I feel hope that I will have a bright future, and I am proud to be black. When I meet a white person who gives me respect and treats me like an equal, I treat him the way he treats me, but that does not mean I wish to be like him. I wish to be just like I am.

CHRONOLOGY

1948 The National Party comes to power in South Africa and begins implementing apartheid.

1955 The African National Congress and others create the Freedom Charter.

1958 Hendrik Verwoerd becomes prime minister of South Africa.

1960 Police kill sixty-nine protesters in Sharpeville; Albert Lutuli wins the Nobel Peace Prize.

1962 The United Nations calls for economic sanctions against South Africa.

1963 Nelson Mandela is sentenced to life in prison.

1966 Verwoerd is assassinated.

1976 Hundreds are killed in riots in the black Johannesburg township Soweto.

1984 Desmond Tutu wins the Nobel Peace Prize.

1989 F.W. de Klerk takes power and calls for a nonracist South Africa.

1990 De Klerk releases Mandela from prison.

1991   The Harare Declaration—a historic and influential document setting forth guidelines to peacefully end apartheid—is signed.

1993   The United Nations ends economic sanctions against South Africa; Mandela and de Klerk share the Nobel Peace Prize.

1994   Mandela is elected president; the African National Congress wins control of the legislature.

1995   The Truth and Reconciliation Commission is established.

1999   Mandela retires as president.

FOR FURTHER READING

Books

James L. Gibson, *Overcoming Apartheid: Can Truth Reconcile a Divided Nation?* New York: Russell Sage Foundation, 2004.

Robert Harvey, *The Fall of Apartheid: The Inside Story from Smuts to Mbeki.* New York: Palgrave Macmillan, 2003.

Adam Hochschild, *The Mirror at Midnight: A South African Journey.* New York: Viking Penguin, 1990.

Alex La Guma, ed., *Apartheid: A Collection of Writings on South African Racism by South Africans.* New York: International, 1971.

A.J. Luthuli, *Let My People Go.* New York: McGraw-Hill, 1962.

Mark Mathabane, *Kaffir Boy: The True Story of a Black Youth's Coming of Age in Apartheid South Africa.* New York: Macmillan, 1986.

David Mermelstein, ed., *The Anti-Apartheid Reader: The Struggle Against White Racist Rule in South Africa.* New York: Grove Press, 1987.

A. N. Pelzer, ed., *Verwoerd Speaks: Speeches 1948–1966.* Johannesburg: APB, 1966.

Jan Christian Smuts, *The Basis of Trusteeship.* Johannesburg: South African Institute of Race Relations, 1942.

Desmond Mpilo Tutu, *Hope and Suffering; Sermons and Speeches.* Grand Rapids, MI: Eerdmans, 1984.

Periodicals

Barry Bearak, "Post-Apartheid South Africa Enters Anxious Era," *The New York Times*, October 6, 2008.

Ken Booth and Peter Vale, "Security in Southern Africa: After Apartheid, Beyond Realism," *International Affairs*, vol. 71, no. 2, April 1995.

Andrew Brackenbury, "South Africa: The Long Walk Continues," *Geographical*, vol. 76, no. 4, April 2004.

Ruth M. Brice, "Apartheid: Financed in the USA," *USA Today,* September 11, 1989.

John de St. Lorre, "South Africa Embattled," *Foreign Affairs*, vol. 65, no. 3, 1986.

Kenneth R. Dombroski, "South Africa After Apartheid," *Journal of Democracy*, vol. 17, no. 3, July 2006.

Cameron Doudo, "Who Will Save South Africa?" *New African*, vol. 475, July 2008.

Peter Duignan, "The Future of South Africa: Will It Be Violent or Peaceful?" *Vital Speeches of the Day*, vol. 56, no. 15, May 15, 1990.

Nigel Gibson, "The Pitfalls of South Africa's 'Liberation,'" *New Political Science*, vol. 23, no. 3, September 2001.

Thomas W. Hazlett, "Economic Origins of Apartheid," *Contemporary Policy Issues*, vol. 6, no. 4, October 1988.

Zenzile Khumalo, "Politics of Inclusion," *New African*, vol. 443, August/September 2005.

Nelson Mandela, "A Formula to End Apartheid," *Human Rights: Journal of the Section of Individual Rights and Responsibilities*, vol. 17, no. 3, Fall/Winter 1990.

Lorna McGregor, "Individual Accountability in South Africa: Cultural Optimum or Political Facade?" *The American Journal of International Law*, vol. 95, no. 1, January 2001.

Bob Minzesheimer, "How Mandela Won Over a Nation," *USA Today*, August 14, 2008.

Hasu Patel, "Southern Africa and Democracy in the Light of the Harare Declaration," *Round Table*, vol. 89, no. 357, October 2000.

"Public and Private Sanctions Against South Africa," *Political Science Quarterly*, vol. 109, no. 2, Summer 1994.

Maano F. Ramutsindela and David Simon, "The Politics of Territory and Place in Post-apartheid South Africa: The Disputed Area of Bushbuckridge," *Journal of Southern African Studies*, vol. 25, no. 3, September 1999.

Krisztina Thanyi, "Racial Integration in the USA and South Africa: Lessons in a Comparative Perspective," *International Journal of Inclusive Education*, vol. 11, no. 2, March 2007.

Michael West, "Mobilizing New Constituencies for Africa," *Black Scholar*, vol. 29, no. l, Spring 1999.

Christopher S. Wren, "Now, to Negotiate the Contours of Apartheid's End," *New York Times*, February 18, 1990.

Lu Zhengrong, "Important Event of the Century," *Beijing Review*, vol. 37, no. 20, May 16, 1994.

Web Sites

Digital Innovation South Africa (www.disa.ukzn.ac.za). DISA is a Web site of scholarly materials related to the freedom struggle in South Africa. Parts of the initiative were funded by the Andrew W. Mellon Foundation.

F.W. de Klerk Foundation (www.fwdklerk.org.za). The F.W. de Klerk Foundation was established in 2000 with the goal of promoting peace in multicommunity states. The Web site contains historic as well as contemporary documents, speeches, and publications to support its mission.

Nelson Mandela Foundation (www.nelsonmandela.org). The Nelson Mandela Foundation, through its Centres of Memory and Dialogue, contributes to the making of a just society by promoting the values, vision, and work of Nelson Mandela. The Web site provides access to the speeches, publications, and other works of Nelson Mandela.

South Africa Institute on Race Relations (www.sairr.org.za). The South Africa Institute on Race Relations is the leading independent research and policy organization in South Africa. The institute publishes widely on education, the economy, business, employment, crime, demographics, health, welfare, and politics. Much of its research can be accessed on the Web site.

INDEX

Abolition of Passes and Co-ordination of
Documents Act of 1952 and, 31–32
farming, 15, 96, 187, 193–197
Industrial Conciliation Act of 1956 and,
30–31
influx control, 22–23, 31–32
mining industry, 143
Native Laws Amendment Act of 1952 and,
31–32
protests and, 23
restrictions on nonwhites, 4
Energy crisis, 138
Ethiopia, 81, 130
Extension of University Education Act of 1959,
30

F

Fanon, Frantz, 119, 120
Farming, 15, 96, 187, 193–197
Farming-on-the-half, 15
Federation of Afrikaner Cultural Organizations
(FAK), 16
Financial Times (newspaper), 109
Food shortages, 130
France, 167
Free market capitalism, 117
Free State, 160
Freedom Charter of African National Congress
(ANC), 23, 69, 118
Freedom Front, 127
Fugard, Athol, 99

G

Gambari, Ibrahim A., 56, 60
Gandhi, Mahatma, 66, 175
Gangs, 191–192
Gender parity, 147
Ghana, 81
Gibson, Nigel, 117–120
Gildenhuys, Anthony, 59
Gold, 14, 21, 142–143
Gordimer, Nadine, 98
Gqozo, Oupa, 124
Graft, 138

Gramsci, Antonio, 119
Great Britain
Afrikaners and, 14–16, 122, 166
Argentina and, 88
Boer War and, 14–15, 21, 122
Botha and, 15
British policy in Africa and, 83–84
control of South Africa, 14–15, 32, 73
racial issues in, 83–84
Smuts and, 15
Great Trek, 14, 16
Group Areas Act of 1950, 28, 29
"Guguletu Seven" incident, 101

H

Hall, John, 59
Harris, Betty J., 13–26
Healthcare, 138, 150–151
Hensoppers, 122
Hertzog, J.B.M., 15
Homelands, 20
Huguenots, 167
Human rights, 62–63, 105–106, 181
Human Rights Day 1959, 68, 70
Hunter College, 85

I

Identification
Abolition of Passes and Co-ordination of
Documents Act of 1952 and, 31–32
crime and, 32
pass laws and, 17, 23
IFP (Inkatha Freedom Party), 59, 104, 114, 182
Imbizos, 136
Immorality Act of 1950, 29
Imprisonment
"Declaration on Apartheid and its Destructive
Consequences in Southern Africa" and, 42
Mandela and, 4, 26
political prisoners, 151–153, 165
In the Heart of the Country (Coetzee), 99
Indentured servants, 14, 17
Indian people
ANC Youth League and, 17
"black consciousness" and, 175